Daughters of Mary Help of Christians
Villa Madonna
315 West Columbus Drive
Tampa, Florida 33602

**A PARAPHRASE OF
THE 16 DOCUMENTS OF VATICAN II**

The Dynamic Voice of Vatican II

Marina E. Ruffolo
General Editor

Rev. John R. Welsh, S.J.
Associate Editor

"Relevance of the Council Today"
by
Cardinal Pericle Felici

ST. PAUL EDITIONS

NIHIL OBSTAT:
Reverend Harold Bumpus
Censor Librorum

IMPRIMATUR:
✠ **Most Reverend Charles B. McLaughlin, D.D.**
Bishop of St. Petersburg

In preparing the paraphrase of each document the contributors and editors made extensive use of these works:
The Documents of Vatican II, general editor, Rev. Walter M. Abbott, S.J.; America Press, 1966
Vatican Council II, general editor, Rev. Austin Flannery, O.P.; Costello Publishing Co., 1975
I Documenti Del Concilio Vaticano II, Edizioni Paoline, 1966
Quotations from the Old and New Testaments are taken from *The New American Bible,* c 1970, used herein by permission of the Confraternity of Christian Doctrine, copyright owner.
Also used in preparation of the work:
Sacrosanctum Oecumenicum Concilium Vaticanum II Constitutiones Decreta Declarationes, Cura et Studio Secretariae Generalis Concilii Oecumenici Vaticani II; Typis Polyglottis Vaticanis, 1966

ISBN 0-8198-0405-3 cloth
ISBN 0-8198-0406-1 paper

Library of Congress Cataloging in Publication Data

The Dynamic voice of Vatican II.

1. Vatican Council, 2d, 1962-1965. I. Ruffolo, Marina E. II. Welsh, John Robert, 1926-
III. Felici, Pericle. The relevance of the Council today. 1977. IV. Vatican Council. 2d, 1962-1965.
BX830.1962.D9   262'.001   77-22673

Copyright © 1980, 1977, by the Daughters of St. Paul

Printed in U.S.A. by the Daughters of St. Paul
50 St. Paul's Ave., Boston, Ma. 02130

The Daughters of St. Paul are an international religious congregation serving the Church with the communications media.

*To His Holiness Pope Paul VI
who amidst bitter tribulations
with untiring love and enduring courage
led us out of a world submersed
in darkness toward that
"light which knows no setting"*
          (Lumen Gentium).
          Marina Ruffolo

Contents

Preface	9
Acknowledgements	14
Relevance of the Council Today	
Cardinal Pericle Felici	15
Message to Humanity	25
Declaration on Religious Freedom	
Rev. Norman J. Rogge, S.J., and	
Rev. John R. Welsh, S.J.	29
Pastoral Constitution on the Church in the Modern World	
Rev. John R. Welsh, S.J.	41
Dogmatic Constitution on Divine Revelation	
Rev. E. J. Jacques, S.J.	89
Dogmatic Constitution on the Church	
Marina E. Ruffolo	101
Constitution on the Liturgy	
Rev. C. J. McNaspy, S.J.	143
Decree on Eastern Catholic Churches	
Rev. Robert Ference	159
Decree on Ecumenism	
Rev. Harold B. Bumpus	167
Declaration on the Relationship of the Church to Non-Christian Religions	
Rev. Austin N. Park, S.J.	179
Decree on the Apostolate of the Laity	
Rev. Harold B. Bumpus	183
Decree on the Church's Missionary Activity	
Rev. Simon E. Smith, S.J.	209
Decree on the Bishops' Pastoral Office in the Church	
Rev. Gregory J. Andrews	225
Decree on the Life and Ministries of Priests	
Mr. Robert Gibbons	243
Decree on the Appropriate Renewal of the Religious Life	
Sister M. Jerome Leavy, O.S.B., and	
Sister Mary Gregoria Rush, O.S.F.	259
Decree on Priestly Formation	
Rev. Sidney A. Lange, S.J.	269
Declaration on Christian Education	
Rev. Thomas M. Kelly, S.J.	281
Decree on the Instruments of Social Communication	
Rev. Frederick J. Buckley	289
The Contributors	297

PREFACE

Bishops and patriarchs, cardinals and theologians of the Roman Catholic Church gathered by hundreds and thousands in St. Peter's Basilica in Vatican City. It was October 11, 1962, the start of the greatest event in recent history of the Church: the Second Ecumenical Council of the Vatican. A full three years later the Council had finished its work and sounded a dynamic message of salvation: a message of what the Church is, what she is called to be and to do, a message of meaning and purpose of human life itself.

When the Church says she works for the salvation of mankind, she wants us to know that she is in watchful, loving service for all men everywhere. All are God's children. All are destined to know Him, love Him, and find their happiness in Him. Especially today the Church sees herself as serving the human person in all that makes him human: soul, body, environment, culture, society. She is concerned with every aspect of human life: the starvation of men, their illness, their despair, technology, violence, whatever evils degrade human dignity, war, world poverty and injustice. And to all that is human the Church brings a saving message of hope.

Just as Christ our Lord long ago fixed His gaze on the earthly city of Jerusalem, wept in anguish over the on-coming woes of His people, and lamented that they "did not know the things that are for their peace"; so does the Church today. Because of her unique position in world affairs, the Church, through her leaders all over the world engaged in every human endeavor, monitors most carefully every movement and trend in secular life, in technological society, and in cultural affairs. With keen insight she knows the impact such developments will have upon human life and their effects within the human spirit, either to enhance or to degrade humanity. True to her mission, which, like Christ's, is a mission to the world, the Church is quick to seize the initiative in pointing out the things "that are for our peace," as well as those trends which are destructive of human welfare and happiness. It was to this task that the Fathers of the Second Vatican Council devoted their talents and energy. Speaking through the Council the Church calls us all with a herald's voice to know what it is the Lord wants of us in today's world.

Let that voice reach the minds and touch the hearts of the faithful, and indeed all men of good will; then will it have the power to bring true peace to the world and enliven humanity with the spirit of Christ's Gospel. Yet because the decrees and documents of Vatican II are lengthy, often technical and presented in unfamiliar terms, for many the Council's voice is muted and silent.

It is in the hope of bringing its dynamic voice to all men that the sixteen documents of the Council have been paraphrased in an easy-to-read version. Like any paraphrase or condensation, this resume of the documents lacks the nuance and subtilty of the originals. It is not intended to be a substitute for the original documents; rather it is our hope that readers will be encouraged to turn to the translations of the documents better prepared to understand and appreciate the treasures of Vatican II.

But how can the Church teach something as true today which she did not teach in earlier times? Such is the question that comes to the minds of many who take a serious look at the sixteen documents of the Second Vatican Council. Behind this question, however, what is often assumed is that the Church now gives expression to a teaching which was never a part of the revealed truth entrusted to her dutiful protection. This assumption ought to be examined.

The Church teaches in a variety of ways with varying degrees of emphasis and clarity and with differing terminology as she addresses herself to questions that have come up in different times in her long history. This variety of expression is usually due to circumstances which push one issue rather than another to the fore. To be specific, the world had to wait until political systems became sufficiently attuned to individual rights and to the full dignity of the human person within the state before the question of religious freedom could be given the form Vatican II gives in its Declaration on Religious Freedom. The Church has not previously taught explicity, "in so many words," and with the careful precision of terminology about this issue as is the case in this document. She did not so teach because the question of religious freedom had not been posed with the urgency or the clarity of insight as has occurred over the last fifty years. For it is only in this century that civil governments have fostered among their citizens genuine political freedom and self-determination. Church teaching often ripens within the climate of human thought as that thought matures. Yet the Church addresses the question of religious freedom, as the Council clearly says, from the basic teaching of the Gospel, a teaching which has perdured in the Church all the centuries of her existence.

The Church, as the faithful teacher of revealed truth entrusted to her by Jesus Christ, must give to any question of faith and morals an answer that is fully consistent with the core of revealed truth. The Gospel message — like a gold mine — is so rich that at no one time is it all seen in its most far-reaching ramifications; and a penetrating probing into the core of truth is possible only when in the course of history the varieties of human experience expose some new vein of thought. So, for example, it has always been part of the Church's mission to teach that the act of faith is the act of a freely affirming mind. But it was not until this century that the question of the right and duty of each person to follow his immediate and properly enlightened conscience in public life was thrown into relief so clearly that popes and bishops could see that the doctrine of "religious freedom" within the state does indeed belong to that true mother lode of revealed truth.

The fact, then, that the Church now teaches clearly and in modern terms something which in earlier times was not fully developed only says to us that she is the divine mystery made up of human beings.

Thus the Church teaches according to the very nature of what she is: human beings who carry the divine in earthen vessels. A so-called "new" teaching is not really a new *truth*, but a development or application of an ancient truth to a modern question. What is new is the linking together of truths long since known but never before joined together with such insight and clarity. That insight and clarity need time to mature. Name it a "new teaching" if you must; but it is not a new truth, in the sense that the Church would now be teaching something which was never before a part of that patrimony of truth entrusted to her by Christ.

We have here the answer to the question, how can the Church teach what she has not taught before. Because the totality of divine truth is inexhaustible, the Church will ever be drawing from what has been revealed to her new conclusions, new applications, new answers, new insights, and new linkages between disparate glimpses of the total truth. As in every human experience new dimensions are always arising, so in religious experience the Church can always discover mirrored back to her from the font of revelation a fresh facet of truth. In speaking of the Holy Spirit our Lord promised, "When he comes, being the Spirit of truth, he will guide you to all truth" (Jn. 16:13).

The Church's teaching is thus an authentic product of the life-giving truth which is in her, namely, Christ and the Holy Spirit.

The Editors

ACKNOWLEDGEMENTS

Though I hesitate to begin a list of those who deserve my thanks, since I could not name each one who in some way has made the book possible, yet certain persons stand out so prominently that I want to mention them with my warmest gratitude: first of all my bishop, the Most Reverend Charles B. McLaughlin, D.D., who encouraged me and guided the work by his wise counsel; Reverend Harold Bumpus, Professor of Catholic Studies at St. Leo College, for his steadfast encouragement, and his outstanding help in all expressions of Catholic theology; Reverend John R. Welsh, S.J., Chairman of the Religion Department of Jesuit High School, who as associate editor worked closely with me at every step of the way; Reverend E.J. Jacques, S.J., Professor of Theology at Spring Hill College, for his help on biblical sections of "Lumen Gentium"; Reverend Larion J. Elliot, S.J., President of Jesuit High School, Tampa, Florida, for his practical advice and for taking in hand so many details required to bring the book to completion; Mrs. Ethel Wilson and Mrs. Bonnie Miller who typed the entire manuscript. No words can pay due tribute to all the contributors, whose names appear in the Table of Contents.

Marina Ruffolo

Relevance of the Council Today

By Cardinal Pericle Felici
President of the Pontifical Commission
for the Revision of the Code of Canon Law

It may seem strange to speak of the Second Vatican Council today. It is simply ten years since it concluded and the work of implementing it is in full development, not only in the doctrinal and disciplinary field but also in the pastoral one. The revision of the Code of Canon Law also, which has now reached the end of its first phase of study, is inspired by the spirit of the Council as well as by its content.

Yet it is necessary to speak of the Council to clarify some ideas, both for those who have always believed this Council to be irrevelevant, as if it had damaged, if not betrayed, the genuine tradition of the Church; and for those who, while they applauded the "openings" of Vatican II (sometimes interpreted for their own private use), subsequently surprised by what they consider to be a reactionary outlook or at least the ultraconservatism of higher ecclesial structures, think they can act on their own, creating other "structures," the nature and purposes of which seem rather to obey an arbitrary transfer of the "deprecated power," to their own advantage. For this reason some people are said to be thinking already of another Ecumenical Council.

To Know Its Teachings

But if we reason serenely, just because the Council has become a sign of contradiction, we see that its relevance is more keenly felt than ever today.

For us pastors and faithful, to make the Council relevant, it is necessary above all to know its teachings. Evidently it is not possible to demand a deep knowledge from everyone. But it is the duty of all those who must follow the directives of the Council to know substantially what they are. It is the strict duty of those who speak in the capacity of scholars, historians and teachers to tell the truth, with the aid of the historical and doctrinal sources, now open to everyone (24 volumes of large format, amounting to 30,000 pages in all, have been published so far), in order not to fall into the danger into which many have fallen, of distorting facts and events and making the Council say what the Council (I say the Council, not a Father or some expert or other) really did not say.

To put the Council into practice, therefore, it is necessary to know it. The doctrine in the first place. As is known, the Council did not wish to propose new dogmas. In some cases, however, in addition to renewing the expression of the content of the perennial Magisterium of the Church, it brought deepening of doctrine, clarification of thought and a more modern style thus consecrating in documents of high value what was already in the wholesome development of the dogma. The Council's is a teaching faithful to the deposit of faith and, at the same time, open to the requirements of our times.

Stress on Man's Dignity

In the practical application, some people may have taken these two characteristics of conciliar teaching as a starting point to take up position on two opposite fronts. However the true doctrine of the Council cannot be blamed for that, just as St. Paul could not be blamed when some points of his teaching, as St. Peter laments, were distorted to sustain theses far-removed from Pauline thought (cf. 2 Pt. 3:16). Moreover, do not some counterfeiters of Christ's doctrine often refer to the Gospel? Do not those who deny the institutional Church refer to the Gospel today? Yet it is written in the Gospel: "You are Peter and on this rock I will build my Church"; and again: "He who listens to you, listens to me; he who despises you, despises me"; and finally: "Feed my sheep."

The doctrine of the Council stresses the dignity of man. Some people have wished to see in this the consecration of a humanism. But there is humanism and humanism. The humanism of the Council is that of Christ who, to carry out the plan of redemption, assumed human nature ennobling the human creature with liberation from sin and with the enrichment of divine life. The leit-motif of the conciliar doctrine on man is taken from the psalm:

"'You made him for a little while lower than the angels;
you crowned him with glory and honor, and put all things under his feet'" (Ps. 8:6; Heb. 2:7, 8).

And is it not holiness, that is, imitation of Christ, the supremely verticalist idea that pervades the whole content of the Council?

Conscience and Freedom

There has been so much discussion recently on man's conscience and freedom also in religious matters. These are difficult subjects which are tackled with different mental attitudes and are therefore solved in diverse ways. The Council dealt with them and those who took part in the lively discussions can realize how, here, too, it is necessary to accept Dante's admonition, with great humility: "Be ye content, O human race, with the *quia!* For if ye had been able to see the whole, no need was there for Mary to give birth" (Purgatorio, III, 37-39). In fact, to the mystery of man is added the mystery of divine economy, so that while on the one hand the Church, teacher of truth, is obliged to preach the good news and have it observed, on the other hand no man can be obliged, I do not say invited, admonished, exhorted, but obliged, to go against his own conscience, once it has been formed well. Moreover, if there were not the free adherence of the will to Christ's own doctrine, there would be neither virtue, nor merit.

The apparent contradiction that some people note in the conciliar Declaration on religious freedom (cf. particularly nn. 1 and 4) is clarified not only by giving the terms (freedom, conscience, evangelization, coercion) their right meaning, but also by setting the teaching on religious freedom in the context of the whole conciliar teaching. This in fact is centered on the mystery of the Trinity, the Incarnation of the Word, Redemption, on the mystery of the Church, which, a pilgrim on earth, is moving towards the heavenly Jerusalem, to which all men are called. And for this reason, while respecting the intimate sanctuary of the individual conscience, the obligation that all the redeemed have to spread the Gospel must not be neglected, nor, consequently, the missionary inspiration and impetus characteristic of the Church, which is sent all over the world, so that all men may believe in God and in the one sent by God, Christ the Lord, the first great Missionary, so that all may be one as the Father and the Son are in the Holy Spirit.

This mission is exercised in the world. The Council dedicated a specific document to the subject: the Pastoral Constitution *Gaudium et Spes*. It must be studied and meditated as a whole and in the context of the entire conciliar teaching, particularly the Constitution *Lumen Gentium* on the Church.

It is useful, sometimes necessary, to dialogue with the men of our time. But it must be done with wisdom, prudence and insight. In any case, dialogue cannot remain an end in itself. We must pass to work, to action, which is certainly more difficult than words, but can actualize the Council with unique efficacy. "...all that Jesus did and taught" (Acts 1:2): the testimony of action preceded his teaching. St. James admonishes: "Act on this word. If all you do is listen to it, you are deceiving yourselves" (1:22). This is a model to be imitated, a teaching to be followed.

Liturgical Phenomenon

Some reflections, finally, on what I would call the "post conciliar liturgical phenomenon." We sometimes hear of a "Mass of Pius V" and a "Mass of Paul VI," as if they contradicted each other both in structure and in language.

In the meantime, there is neither a "Mass of Pius V" nor a "Mass of Paul VI." Substantially the Mass is one only, it is that of Our Lord, who sacrificed Himself for our salvation and, on the eve of His passion and death, instituted the Eucharist as a memorial of His death for our nourishment. This Mass was celebrated from the time of the Apostles throughout the whole course of the history of the Church and will be celebrated until the end of the world.

But by Mass is understood also the set of prayers, spiritual elevations, readings and ceremonies that accompany the essential rite, explaining its significance as sacrifice and as spiritual Communion.

Well, this set has had different expressions and manifestations at various times and according to the various rites. Without mentioning the many Oriental rites or even the different forms of the Latin rite, we must say that the stage providentially marked after the Council of Trent by Pius V, is one of the stages, but not the only one. The Missal of Pius V itself has been revised at different times: we are thinking particularly of the revisions made by Pius X and above all by Pius XII, who rearranged, among other things, the rite of the Holy Week in its entirety. Why should the Council, why should Paul VI not have been able to give a new structure, more adapted to recent liturgical studies and above all more in keeping with the modern pastoral requirements, which emerged from

Vatican II? Unfortunately there have been abuses of varying gravity; but can they be attributed to the content of the Council or to the decrees of Paul VI? The argument brought forward above, returns. Poisonous mushrooms growing at the foot of a sturdy oak, are not the fruit of the oak!

And let us talk a little of Latin. The person who writes this is not a professional, but a modest artisan of the language of Latium and he always expressed himself in this language as Secretary General in the conciliar sessions. So what I am about to say cannot be accused of partiality.

The Council, accepting the wishes of a great many pastors and faithful, established that more space should be given to the spoken or vernacular language, especially in the didactic parts of the Mass. Certainly, the conciliar provision, when put into practice in the reform, had particular determinations. But can it be said that they went against the spirit of the Council?

Using the Vernacular

Let me recall a fact. While the work of the Commission for the implementation of the liturgical Constitution, of which I was a member, was being carried out, a special session was held in a religious Institute near St. Peter's, where in the presence of the members of the Commission an "experimental" Mass was celebrated entirely in Italian, except for the Canon or the central part of the Canon—I don't remember clearly. The discussion followed, in the meeting hall.

One Father said that he had liked the Mass, but he did not understand why the central part, too, had not been said in Italian. I pointed out, on my side, that it was necessary in the first place to establish the criterion for well-regulated use of the spoken language; if the criterion were that the people should understand more, as the Council seemed to have suggested for the didactic parts, no difficulties could be seen about saying also the central part of the Mass in the spoken language, so that the people would understand it better, all the more so since Jesus Himself, speaking the sacramental words which are transmitted to us by the Gospel in Greek, had used Aramaic, the language He and the Apostles spoke. If, however, the criterion was to give the Latin rite also linguistic unity in the essential part, then things would have to remain as they were. I was not surprised, therefore, when the Pope authorized the use of the spoken language also in the whole of the Canon. Provision has been made, furthermore, for the unity of the rite with the typical edition in Latin, by which all the translations must abide, and with the authorization granted to all to celebrate in Latin, where pastoral requirements do not call for another solution. Of course, in practice great care and circumspection are necessary.

Love and Obedience

I end with a reflection. We sometimes feel elated at the new forms of liturgy; and we are right. But we must also remember that the liturgy with which Christ saved the world was made up of love and obedience, and the great sacrificial gesture was marked by two bleeding arms, nailed onto the cross: Yes, Father!

Vatican II finds relevance and realization in love and obedience.

From *L'Osservatore Romano*, January 13, 1977 issue.

Message to Humanity

(Issued at the beginning of the Second Vatican Council by its Fathers, with the endorsement of the Supreme Pontiff.)

"At the direction of...Pope John XXIII, we successors of the Apostles have gathered here, joined in singlehearted prayer with Mary the Mother of Jesus and forming one apostolic body headed by the successor of Peter.... In this assembly, under the guidance of the Holy Spirit, we wish to inquire how we ought to renew ourselves, so that we may be found increasingly faithful to the Gospel of Christ.... Coming together in unity from every nation under the sun, we carry in our hearts the hardships, the bodily and mental distress, the sorrows, longings and hopes of all the peoples entrusted to us. We urgently turn our thoughts to all the anxieties by which modern man is afflicted. Hence, let our concern swiftly focus first on all those who are especially lowly, poor and weak. Like Christ, we would have pity on the multitude weighed down with hunger, misery and lack of knowledge. We want to fix a steady gaze on those who still lack the opportune help to achieve a way of life worthy of human beings. As we undertake our work, therefore, we would emphasize whatever concerns the dignity of man....

"The Supreme Pontiff, John XXIII, in a radio message delivered on September 11, 1962, stressed two points especially.

"The first dealt with *peace* between peoples. There is no one who does not hate war, no one who does not strive for peace with burning desire. But the Church desires it most of all because she is mother of all... she never ceases to make open declarations of her love for *peace,* her desire for *peace.* She strives with all her might to bring peoples together and to develop among men a mutual respect for interest and feelings. This very conciliar congress of ours, so impressive in the diversity of races, nations and languages it represents, does it not bear witness to a community of brotherly love, and shine as a visible sign of it? We are giving witness that all men are brothers, whatever their race or nation.

"The Supreme Pontiff also pleads for social justice...the Church is supremely necessary for the modern world if injustices...are to be denounced, and if the order of...values is to be restored, so that man's life can become more human according to the standards of the Gospel."

Declaration on Religious Freedom

(Dignitatis Humanae, December 7, 1965)

A paraphrase by
Rev. Norman J. Rogge, S.J.
and Rev. John R. Welsh, S.J.

The Right of the Person and of Communities to Social and Civil Freedom in Religious Matters

1. In modern times mankind is becoming ever more conscious of the dignity of the human person. Essential to that dignity is that a person act in responsible freedom. More and more in our times people are demanding that they be able to act on their own judgments out of a sense of duty and not from compulsion, and so are requiring that Constitutional limits should be set to the powers of government not to hinder their rightful freedom as persons and as social groups. The exercise of this freedom affects all the values of the human spirit, but chiefly the practice of religion.

Aware that the desire for personal freedom is in full accord with truth and justice, we, the Fathers of this Council, intend to address religious freedom from the vantage point of traditional Church teaching. Basic to this teaching is the two-fold truth: God has told the human race how He intends all to serve Him and find salvation in Jesus Christ, His Son; and it is to the Catholic and apostolic Church that Christ assigned the duty of spreading the light of salvation (Mt. 28:19-20). Also, every human person has the duty to seek the truth and to live up to that truth, especially as it concerns God and His Church.

It is through his conscience that each person fulfills this duty as the truth discloses itself to each by its own power. Religious freedom, as the means one needs to find the truth and act on it, sets one free from any external compulsion. Hence, the moral duty of each and all toward religion and the true Church of Christ remains in full force. In line with recent Papal teaching we will develop the notion of religious freedom as a right of all persons and an obligation of civil society for their protection.

CHAPTER I

2. We affirm the right of religious freedom for human persons, which means that no one is to be forced to act against what he believes, nor prevented from acting in accordance with his beliefs, either publicly or privately, whether alone or with others. Moreover, the basis for this right is the very dignity of being a person, as we know it from reason and from the Word of God. The right of religious freedom should be a part of the laws of all nations and become a civil right.

All persons have an inborn desire to find truth and so have a natural duty to seek it, especially religious truth. They do so because all have the power to reason and to make free choices; following upon this, they are responsible for living up to their convictions about the truth they have discovered.

The only way people can be responsible for their own judgments is to enjoy a genuine freedom from coercive force. This is why religious freedom must be safeguarded for all persons regardless of their honesty in living up to their duty to find the truth. It is based on the fact that each one is to be responsible for his own activity, and in particular for his search for truth.

3. There is another consideration. Through His divine wisdom which is eternal and unchanging God continually governs all things in the universe, and in a special way the human race. Mankind perceives the directives of His wisdom and discovers in His will the truths by which human life is ordered to its highest goal, God Himself. It is for each one, then, to seek religious truth and the only manner of seeking truth that befits the dignity of the human person is a free inquiry. This means that after diligent, authentic instruction and communication with one another in the search for truth, a person draws his own conclusion his search has disclosed to him. Quite simply, a person must faithfully follow his conscience to come to God. Consequently, no one is to be forced to act against conscience, nor restrained from acting as it dictates. And since acts of religion consist in the free, internal activity of a person in communion with God, no power on earth may interfere with, command, nor prohibit them. Moreover man is social by nature and by openly professing their beliefs in joint action with others human beings mirror externally the religious beliefs of the human spirit. And these external actions must be free from coercion; otherwise the proper functioning of human life as intended by God would be frustrated.

Then again, governments must provide for the total welfare of their citizens; but the religious activity of people leads them to the supreme welfare of human life itself. Thus it is that governments must provide for the free exercise of religion without attempting to either inhibit or impose religious activity.

4. When people join together for the practice of religion, their association deserves the right to be free and secure from coercive force. This is so because all men need the freedom to unite with others in groups. As long as they do not sow discord among their fellow citizens, these groups should be free to govern themselves, worship God publicly, instruct their believers, and set up organizations for promoting their religious ideals.

Governments must not interfere with nor hinder a religious group in the selection, training, and assignment of its ministers; in its contacts with religious leaders in other countries, nor in its acquiring and use of its own property.

It would be against the rights of religious groups if a government should prevent them from spreading their teachings among other citizens. But in doing this religious groups must not abuse their own rights nor infringe upon the rights of others. This means that they are to avoid anything like pressuring others to become believers.

Moreover religious freedom should safeguard the right of religious groups to speak out on public issues as their religious convictions prompt them. Finally the social nature of man and the very nature of religion warrants the right of men to freely establish educational, cultural, charitable social organizations springing from their own religious sense.

5. The family unit has the right to live freely it own religious life. Therefore parents have the

right to provide for their children an education in religion which they freely choose. This right is to be protected by every civil government nor may unjust burdens be imposed on parents who exercise this right. It would be a clear violation if children are forced to attend lessons that go against their beliefs, or if they must attend only those schools which omit religious training.

6. The very reason people form a society is that in this way the benefits of an association may be shared by all people more easily than if each acted on his own. Among the chief benefits of any society is that it protects the rights of people and helps them carry out their duties. Thus, promoting religious freedom for people is the shared responsibility of all who make up a society — government, social groups, and churches.

The protection of inviolable rights of all ranks among the essential duties of governments. Let them, then, foster religious freedom of citizens both by laws and by creating a climate favorable to the practice of religion. All society, indeed, profits from the qualities of justice and peace which flow from man's faithfulness to God.

It can happen that due to circumstances a government gives special legal standing to one religious group above all others. Yet that government must assure the rights of all other groups to religious freedom. The equality of every citizen before the law must be carefully protected from any kind of religious discrimination.

Accordingly, it is seriously wrong for any government to compel its people to adopt or reject a religion, or to join or leave a religious group. The condition in which civil authorities repress religion in a country or on an international scale is a serious violation of God's Will and the rights of humanity.

7. Any time people use their freedom in society they must weigh it against the rights and duties of their fellow citizens. Personal and social responsibility dictate that each one treat others justly with an eye on the common welfare.

It is for governments to set up by just laws whatever protection for citizen rights are needed against clear abuses of freedom, such as may happen in matters of religion. The one fair way of doing this is for governments to make their laws according to the norms of justice, for the protection of rights of citizens and the orderly settlement of disputes. For justice among men is founded on the human need for genuine public order and a care for public morality. More generally, let this rule stand: respect freedom as far as possible, curb it only when really necessary.

8. Because of many pressures of our day, people can easily lose a proper balance between freedom and responsibility. The result is that many use the name of freedom as a pretense to oppose authority or to shirk their duty. For our part, we call on whoever has a part to play in the education of people: form them in a love of justice and a whole-hearted response to their duties as citizens. This will make of them true lovers of freedom, that is, persons who make their own judgments based on truth, and who act out of a sense of responsibility for promoting justice for all mankind, willing always to join with others in cooperative efforts.

CHAPTER II

Religious Freedom in the Light of Revelation

9. Our teaching is that the dignity of the human person demands that each one have the right to religious freedom. The experience of centuries have made mankind more aware of all that his dignity demands, and the concept of religious freedom is rooted in divine revelation itself. For revelation does disclose the full dignity of the human person. The model for all His followers is Christ who showed all respect for the freedom of people faced with the duty to believe the Word of God and to give a free assent in the act of faith.

10. Since each one must give to God a response that is free, no one is to be forced against his will. It is founded in Scripture (cf. Jn. 6:44) and in the constant teaching of the Church that the act by which men believe in God is of its very nature a free act. It follows of course that the right to religious freedom fits well with the freedom of the act of faith and fosters excellent opportunities for the spread of the Christian Gospel.

11. God lovingly regards the dignity of the human persons whom He created. He holds each to act as conscience dictates, but freely without coercion. Consider Christ, who is Lord and yet meek and humble, Christ who patiently drew disciples to Himself and by teaching and miracles stirred up their faith in Him, Christ who rebuked

those who refused to believe, yet left all judgment for their disbelief to God at the end of time. This is the Christ who rejected force and might and instead became the servant of all (Mk. 10:45) to die for the redemption and true freedom of all humankind. His Kingdom He founded on the knowledge of the truth, not on force; He draws all to Himself by the power of His love.

In their work to convert men to the Gospel the Apostles followed the Master's example. They relied on the power of the Word of God alone, for they believed that in His Word was the power of God which could destroy all the forces of evil arrayed against it. Though they proclaimed that "God wants all men to be saved and come to know the truth" (1 Tm. 2:4), they taught that each is bound to obey his conscience in coming to faith. Their work was powerful in God because they had confidence in the Gospel message (cf. Rom. 1:16) and its power to bring men to faith in Christ (cf. 2 Cor. 10:3-5). Though they preached obedience to the legitimate authority of the State (Rom. 13:1-5), yet they spoke boldly against rulers who made demands contrary to God's Will (cf. Acts 4:19-20).

12. In endorsing the principle of religious freedom as befits the dignity of each person, the Church is following the footsteps of Christ and His Apostles. No one is to be forced into faith: this has been His constant teaching, even though in practice there have been times in history when the actions of churchmen were out of step with the Gospel. In spite of this, the Gospel has so influenced human culture that in the course of time men

have come more widely to recognize their dignity as persons and so require freedom in matters religious.

13. The most basic demand the Church makes for herself is that she be free to work for the salvation of mankind. So sacred is this freedom to the Church that to act contrary to it would be to oppose God's will. This is fundamental for all relations between the Church and secular governments. There are two reasons for this freedom proper to the Church. The first is the unique spiritual authority of the Church, which comes from Christ's command that she preach the Gospel to all the world (cf. Mk. 16:15); the second is that the Church as a society of persons has the natural right to exist in freedom.

Both in law and in actual practice the Church needs full security for her independence; for only in this way can she carry out her mission of salvation. Christian people, too, have their civil rights to live according to their consciences. It is for these reasons that the freedom of the Church is in full harmony with the right to religious freedom of persons and groups.

14. "Make disciples of all the nations" (Mt. 28:19): this is the command of Christ to His Church that she reach out to all with the light of truth. Christian people are bound to form their consciences by the certain doctrine of the Church which has the backing of Christ's own authority. Included must be the truths about man's inner life and his life in society. Let Christians become bold apostles working to shed this light of Christ upon all they meet. For this they must know

their faith, defend it, and actively promote it — always in the spirit of the Gospel — with prudence and patience in all their dealings with their fellowmen, mindful of each one's rights and the call of God's grace to an expression of faith that is free.

15. People of our age want their freedom in religious matters and increasingly are making this right a constitutional right.

Nevertheless, governments do exist which deny this right to their citizens and actively oppose the practice of religion. We denounce this sad state of affairs and urge all to do what they can to promote religious freedom for the whole human family.

It is fully evident that peoples of the earth are becoming more united and more responsible. But they must have constitutional guarantees which are effective and which fully respect their highest duty and right — to practice religion publicly with full freedom.

May the heavenly Father of us all help mankind to grow through the practice of religious freedom to the "glorious freedom of the children of God" (Rom. 8:21).

Pastoral Constitution on the Church in the Modern World

(Gaudium et Spes, December 7, 1965)

A paraphrase by
Rev. John R. Welsh, S.J.

Preface:
The Bonds Between the Church and the Family of Man

1. The joys, hopes, griefs and anxieties of the human family are the same for all of us who follow Christ. For we Christians, as those who strive for the Kingdom of God and live by the Gospel of Jesus Christ, are bound by every human tie with all of humanity.

2. Now addressing the whole of humanity, we long to explain what we think the presence and activity of the Church entails in today's world. First, we take a careful look at the world itself, the theatre of mankind's history; fallen into the bondage of sin this world of humanity struggles to be free of evil. We believe that it has in truth been liberated in Christ and is called to reach its fulfillment according to God's plan.

3. We see all of humanity desperately struggling with the profound questions of the human person's place in the universe and his ultimate destiny. And to witness our loving solidarity with the human family we engage in a concerned conversation about these very questions which humanity itself raises. Because the Church has rich resources of divine wisdom, we will share these as we center our attention on the preservation and renewal of humanity itself and of all that makes up human dignity. In the same spirit of Christ, who came to serve and witness to the truth, we offer all that the Church can do to further human brotherhood and human dignity.

Introduction:
The Condition
of the Human Family

4.-5. If we would respond according to the light of the Gospel to the ever-recurring questions of humanity about itself, we must first understand our world and listen to what it says to us. Profound and rapid changes are transforming man's view of himself, his society, and culture with important impact on his activity and on religion as well. These vast changes within his life, activity, and power over the world leave men bewildered regarding the direction of it all. On the one hand there are growing aspirations toward abundance, knowledge and unity; and yet on the other the world is plunged in want, illiteracy and war. In this conflict of forces and values, where material progress leaves the spirit impoverished, humanity is forced to ask very fundamental questions about its meaning and its goal on this planet. Indeed vast scientific advances and the rapid progress of technology have made man the master of natural forces of the world in ways undreamed of before our age. And all of this has brought our race to a wholly new concept of the world, one that is more dynamic and evolutionary.

6. This can be clearly seen in the speedy and varied changes in the ways humankind lives together in society: most nations are more industrialized, more urban, more mobile, more affected by rapid communications. Indeed such progress affects peoples

and nations world-wide, impelling them to greater independence in governing themselves.

7. Accepted values are challenged on all fronts: in schools, in law, in traditions, and in religion. Philosophies which ignore God strongly influence literature, the arts, and humanistic education. Many are finding strong resources in their faith and so their practice of religion is deepened and purified. But many others find themselves so shaken in their former belief that they abandon religion and God.

8. The widespread contradictions growing out of too rapid change are intensifying the divisions within individuals and within the human family. Unable to cope with such an array of data and ideas, men grope their way between practical efficiency and the demands of conscience, and between common responsibility and personal growth. Discord mars family relations as well as relations between races, and between national groups and socio-economic classes. Man is both the cause and the victim of such distrust and conflict.

9. In the midst of such confusion there burns steady in men's hearts the determination to develop for humanity around the world a freer and fuller life in the political, economic, and cultural realms. Humanity yearns for a world order befitting the dignity and freedom of all persons, an order in which aspirations for equality are respected and the resources of the world truly benefit all. Yet deep anxiety persists that forces newly unleashed may just as easily enslave humanity

as promote its welfare. Thus men feel the urgency of directing these forces intelligently for genuine progress, especially with regard to developing nations.

10. Humanity is being pulled apart within its inmost being by conflicting attractions: aware of its limitations yet conscious of its boundless desires, weighed down by sin, material greed and woe, man either hopes for human betterment from his own resources or despairs of finding any genuine meaning of human existence. Yet for most there is a profound searching for the meaning of our humanity in this universe. To this questioning the Church offers that light which alone can give mankind the strength and resolve to attain its high destiny, that steady and unfailing light of Christ who is the same yesterday and today, yes and forever.

PART 1
The Church and Mankind's Destiny

11. What is human life? From the way the Church replies it will become clear what genuine service to humanity she can offer. This service will be to assess from the light of faith true human values and relate these to their divine source, from which comes man's dignity and vocation in this world.

CHAPTER I
The Dignity of Human Persons

12. Our starting point for recognizing mankind's dignity and its true situation is that humanity is created to "the image of

God." From this truth we affirm that human persons can know and love their Creator, that they are themselves creators of their world, and that by nature they are in personal relationship with one another.

13. The fact of sin and chaos in the world is explained by man's divorcing himself from the will of God, and from this stems his disharmony with the world and divisions within his own heart. Relying on its own efforts humanity cannot cast away the nets of its sinfulness. Divine truth throws its redeeming light on this plight of humanity: God calling all to the heights, yet sin keeping all bound in misery.

14. We recognize the marvelous dignity of the human body, and realize that human life rises above the whole of visible creation by virtue of the spiritual and immortal soul in each person.

15. By applying the abilities of intellect the human race has won ever greater control over the material world. Then going beyond the data of experiment it has claimed a certainty over greater realms of knowledge. Furthermore, humanity highly values and desperately needs men and women of wisdom, for by this attainment we love what is true and good. By faith and contemplation mankind attains to God Himself.

16. Through conscience, which spurs us to love good and avoid evil, human persons recognize the will of God and can freely respond in keeping with their essential dignity. It is by relying on a correct conscience that we Christians unite most effectively with all men in a common search

for truth and for the solutions to problems of human life. It is according to the honest promptings of conscience that all will be judged.

17. Quite rightly people of our times make much of a person's freedom by which he directs himself to what is good; and freedom is an exceptional sign of a person's participation in the divine image. A person's dignity requires that he act from knowing and free choice, but he must through God's grace gain a freedom from inner constraints, such as passion, in order to pursue worthy goals through proper means. All of us will be judged by our deliberate choices of good or of evil.

18. The riddle of human existence is most clearly evident in death; for man instinctively rejects the notion that he as a person must utterly disappear from the earth. This is true because man is a spiritual being who yearns for a higher life beyond a mere continuation of biological life. Relying on divine revelation we affirm the Christian belief that God destines every person to eternal bliss beyond this earthly misery. That belief assures us that Christ our Savior has won a victory over death in which all persons are called to share. This faith is the foundation of our hopes for a future life with God in eternal happiness.

19. Although human happiness depends upon a personal response of devoted love of God and hence union with Him, there are many who repudiate the very notion of God's existence or affirm that such a notion has no meaning for human understanding. Accordingly atheism is a most serious problem

of our age. An examination of unbelief shows that it takes many forms. Some assert that nothing can be known about God, and are content that "scientific reasoning" alone gives true knowledge or hold that there is no absolute truth available to us. Some so play up human values that they exclude God. Some seem fixed in their indifference to religion. Others make up false notions of what God is and reject these figments in place of the true God. Still others protest against the evil in the world and so deny God. Many who are godless show an almost exclusive concern for earthly affairs. All of these play a part in the several reasons for atheism. Even believers themselves, by their failures to live up to their beliefs or by teaching a false view of God, must share some responsibility for concealing rather than revealing the true face of God and religion.

20. There is in modern times an organized or systematic atheism. This rejection of God is founded on such claims for man's independence that it spurns any dependence on God as being a threat to human freedom. Specifically, such atheistic systems claim that religion diverts human beings from building the earthly city of man, and so they use the power of government to suppress religion.

21. The Church firmly rejects atheism as a corruption of man's dignity; yet realizing that atheists raise very serious questions, she thinks these deserve close examination. We cannot agree that belief in God is hostile to man's dignity, since that dignity is founded in God who bestows it and calls it to perfec-

tion. Not only does a future hope of eternal life not rob earthly duties of their urgency, but it provides the incentive for action in the world and insures humanity against blank despair as well. For only God can fully answer man's ceaseless questing for the full meaning of human life. The fundamental remedy for atheism is the living witness to God by the lives of those who show forth justice, love, compassion and unity with others, which are signs of God's presence. We urge all men, believers and unbelievers alike, to work for the betterment of our common world. We call for sincere dialogue with fully guaranteed respect for the human rights of all persons as the way to achieve this. We encourage all atheists to examine the Gospel message which is fully in harmony with the development of all human values.

22. The true image of the human being, the one who expresses perfectly the mystery and sublime dignity of all humanity, is Christ. By becoming man the Son of God joined His person to human life in all things except sin and by His sacrificial death reconciled the whole race to the Father. Through Him and in likeness to Him all have access to their destiny as children of God. Called in the Spirit of Christ to love his fellowmen and struggle against evil even unto death, the Christian patterns his life on Christ and is united with Him in His resurrected life. Through the mystery of God's grace all human persons are effectively called to share in this same destiny, a vocation to have life and to have it more abundantly.

CHAPTER II
The Community of Mankind

23. Increasingly people of one nation rely upon other people in our world; and this has come about through modern technical advances. Yet its perfection is reached at the level of person-to-person relations. Christian revelation promotes the call to brotherly dialogue by its demand for mutual respect based on human dignity. We will stress the deeper laws of social life and their foundations in man's spiritual nature, and develop their importance for the world of today.

24. In creating us in His image, God has called us to live as one family in a spirit of brotherhood and find our true goal in Him. And so it is that His first and greatest commandment is that we love God and neighbor. "Love is the fulfillment of the law" (Rom. 13:8-10). Realizing how important this message is for human happiness, Jesus prayed that our unity in charity might in a way mirror the unity of the divine Persons of the Trinity (Jn. 17:21-22).

25. As human persons we need to live our lives in the society of other persons, for through this association we develop the deepest yearnings of our nature. Among the most basic of these are the family and political society. Then by our free decisions we also form other organizations within our societies; these carry out the desires we have for a better quality of life as well as for the protection of our rights. Still it cannot be denied that upheavals and tensions in the social

environment tend to corrupt man's noblest desires turning them to evil results. At a deeper level such evils flow from man's pride and selfishness. Only by a constant effort coupled with God's grace can we overcome our sinfulness and the many inducements to sin.

26. The whole human race, interacting according to its rights and duties throughout the world, must be concerned for the common good or general welfare of all. What is this "common good"? It refers to the actual conditions of human life, those conditions which promote in every way the full development of human potential. Where there is a common good, all social groups and their members have ready access to such means for their development as is required by their standing in the human family. And because each of us is a person with human dignity, there must be at hand to each of us all things necessary for living a life that is really human: physical security, rights to free choice in family life, education, employment, rights to respect, to information, to act according to conscience, to privacy and to religious freedom. It follows then that the proper ordering of any society must be directed to benefit the human persons who make it up. It is for this very reason that mankind forms societies. Thus constant improvements and changes in society are demanded to bring it everywhere in line with truth, justice, love and freedom. The guiding Spirit of God working through the Gospel message arouses all of us to build our society to this end.

27. In particular we urge such reverence for one another and for man's life and the means to live in dignity, that each consider the neighbor as another self. And we must see in each the neighbor we can help: the elderly, the abandoned, the foreigner, the migrant, the child born out of wedlock, and the hungry. And on the contrary whatever means are used to destroy human life, or to violate the integrity of the body or the mind or the freedom of man; whatever insults human dignity or degrades the human spirit: all are infamies that harm those who practice them more than their victims. Indeed these things dishonor the Creator.

28. We ought to respect and love those who think and act contrary to our own ways of thinking and acting, and thereby open the door to dialogue with them. And while our love prompts us to speak the truth as we know it, we repudiate all error, but hold in esteem the person who is in error. For God who alone is the searcher of hearts forbids us to judge the guilt of anyone. Christ requires us to forgive injuries and as His command states: "Love your enemies, pray for your persecutors" (Mt. 5:44).

29. We must recognize the basic equality of all: enjoying as we do the same nature and origin, redeemed in Christ and called to the same destiny. Though we differ one from another in many respects, i.e., sex, race, color, language or religion, the basic rights of each person should be protected from every type of discrimination based on non-essential features, for such is contrary to God's intent. Regretably personal rights are not universally

recognized especially in the case of women whose freedom and status are not generally held on a par with those of males. The equal dignity of all persons demands that every economic and social condition that is contrary to social justice and international peace be done away with. Human institutions must fight against the slavery of man, whether social or political; insure the political rights of man, and serve the highest purpose of all, man's spiritual aspirations.

30. We can fulfill the demands of justice and love first by rejecting firmly a morality that looks just at individuals. Next let us all pour our united abilities into a common effort through every human institution with this single aim: the betterment of the human condition in this world. Nevertheless some live as if they cared nothing for the needs of society: they despise laws, avoid taxes and scorn the norms of social living, indifferent to the risk to human life itself. Truly it is the primary duty of each one to pay heed to social needs. In a world in which group action has its repercussions upon the whole race, it is essential that we as individuals and associations refine our moral and social sense toward the building up of a new humanity.

31. The young in every land from every social class must be educated to a high degree of culture, so that from a new generation will come men and women of generous hearts eager for service. Responsible freedom is shackled when those who are to exercise it cannot experience their true dignity due, for instance, to extreme poverty. But when a free person takes up the burdens of responsible

human life, he commits himself to the service of mankind. Praiseworthy indeed are the efforts and procedures of those governments which promote among their people a free sharing in common undertakings. If social groups dedicated to the common welfare would attract and dispose the citizen to serve in common endeavors, they must inspire him with reasons for living and hoping.

32. As is clear from the very start of salvation history, God intends the human race to be saved through their vocation as a people, His own people called to holiness in a covenant with Him. Then too Jesus Christ through the many community ties of His life willed to share in human fellowship. He revealed His Father's love for men both through figures of speech drawn from social life and through His life of obedience to law, the family duty, and to a workman's toil. In His preaching Jesus taught us that we are brothers and the greatest love is "to lay down one's life for one's friends" (Jn. 15:13). After rising from the dead He founded a Family of God based on love, the Church which is His Body, and destined all to find there a perfection of solidarity as brothers in Him.

CHAPTER III

Man's Activity Throughout the World

33. Through science and technology the human race has achieved a mastery over nature that is relatively complete, and through an exchange among nations is making itself

into a single world community. In the face of such benefits, which the race has won for itself by native ability, many raise disturbing questions about the value and use of such achievements and their true goal. Drawing on its reserves of religious and moral truth, the Church wants to shed what light it can upon these choices in human development.

34. Human activity aimed at bettering our lives on this planet has the blessing of God who has given us the command to master and govern all it contains to the glory of God to whom all things are referred. As men and women provide for themselves and their families they are also working for the benefit of society and thus are contributing by their work to the accomplishment of the divine plan. Not only is there no opposition between man's work and God's power, but we as Christians see in all human accomplishment the glory of God; for by extending his power man thereby extends his common responsibility for building the world. True to the Christian message we are bound to work for this very objective.

35. Through our work in the world we develop our inner human resources, which are of greater value than external riches; for real worth belongs to the person rather than to his possessions. A more humane ordering of social relationships is more vital than technical advances, for these latter provide the material for human progress, but they do not constitute progress, which must be judged according to the genuine good for the human race.

36. To set at rest any fear that religion seeks to interfere with the independence of man in his earthly affairs, we affirm that all created things enjoy their own specific laws, laws which mankind can discover by methods appropriate to the various sciences and arts. There is no conflict between faith and genuine scientific investigation, for both have the same God as their author who holds all in existence. So it is that we deplore that attitude which would deny to science its rightful independence. Of course all who believe in God can see that it would be false to assert that created things are independent of God for their existence or that we may use them without reference to God.

37. Human progress brings with it the threatened destruction of humanity. This happens when persons and groups yielding to the temptations of self-interest lose true values and corrupt true brotherhood. The fact is we are ceaselessly caught up in a struggle with the dark forces of evil in which only by effort and the grace of God do we maintain our integrity. Although human progress can serve man's happiness, its price is that we keep progress from becoming an instrument of sin, vanity, and malice. The Christian answer to such threats is the power of Christ's cross and resurrection. For only in Christ can we love created things as God's gift and use them with due reverence. Once we enjoy real freedom of spirit can we truly possess all things. "All things are yours, and you are Christ's and Christ is God's" (1 Cor. 3:22-23).

38. The Word of God in becoming flesh entered the world's history to transform it by

love into the image of Himself, the perfection of humanity. And to all He opens the way of divine love as the foundation of a universal brotherhood to be lived fully in ordinary life. Taught by Christ's example we must shoulder our cross in search for peace and justice. In this struggle we rely on His Spirit which empowers us to strive to make the world more human. In the gifts of this same Spirit we all labor in differing roles: some giving witness to our heavenly goal and others dedicated to the earthly service of the human community. Yet the Spirit frees all from selfishness and inspires all to work for the future of humanity. In the Eucharistic Meal the Lord leaves us a pledge and promise of both brotherly solidarity and of the heavenly banquet.

39. Though we do not know when nor how all things will be transformed, we do believe that God is preparing a new dwelling place for justice, peace, and human blessedness. Then will the sons and daughters of God be raised up and, freed from death and sin, live in everlasting charity. This hope for a future world must not weaken but rather stimulate our concern for building up here and now the future body of the human family. And though earthly progress is not Christ's kingdom; still as it is ordered to human society, it is vital to the Kingdom of God. When at last we the human race have completed our work of nuturing the earthbound values of human dignity, we will find them again freed from dross and transfigured into the eternal Kingdom of Christ.

On this earth that kingdom exists in mystery; on the Lord's day it will be in full flower.

CHAPTER IV
The Church's Role in Modern Life

40. All that has been said regarding the human person, human society, and human activity forms the foundation for what we now teach about the relationship of the Church to the modern world, mindful as we are that the Church is a living and active part of modern history. Although the Church by her divine Founder has the purpose of saving men for a kingdom in the age to come, still her members are called to live and work in the present history of mankind. Since the Church is a visible society of human persons, she shares the same earthly lot of humanity, but as a yeast she labors to transform the world into God's family. And so this mystery, the Church, communicates to all the blessings of divine life: exalting man's dignity, strengthening his societies, and giving deeper meaning to his activities.

The Catholic Church has the greatest esteem for all that other Christian bodies are doing to make our world more truly human. And in truth, the industry of individuals and of human society can help the Church in fostering the Gospel message.

41. In modern life humankind seeks the development of the person and the protection of human rights. Serving the quest of a better humanity, the Church opens to man his real meaning and truth founded in his ulti-

mate goal which is God. She offers an appropriate response to the religious searching of the human heart. Thus the full dignity and freedom of man is aptly safeguarded by the Gospel of Christ. This Gospel calls us to freedom from sin, to the exercise of conscience, and to love for one another. The rightful autonomy of man is established and affirmed by the struggle for the rights of man. The Gospel of Christ fosters this goal and provides through the claims of divine law a safeguard against any kind of false autonomy of man.

42. Through her mission to foster the growth of God's family, the Church gives an impetus to unify human society as a whole through activities meeting human needs. She favors and fosters those movements toward greater union of minds and hearts which are especially evident in civic and economic life. Through the force of practical faith and charity the Church injects into the world of humanity an inner evolution toward unity. Because of her universality the Church can be a real binding force among diverse nations, and she urges all to set aside strife and to cooperate with all just associations of men. We declare that we respect all human societies which foster the just claims of human dignity and that we will work with them all to the extent that is consistent with the Church's mission.

43. All Christians are reminded of their positive obligation to measure up to their earthly responsibilities. It is a most serious error to think that we can live our lives of faith and worship by splitting them off from

moral obligations arising from earthly affairs, or to fulfill our duties in the world divorced from religious duty. If Christians neglect their temporal obligations, they wrong the neighbor and God Himself to their eternal peril. Let them rather imitate Christ, the workman, and by their labor in the world express the religious direction of their lives for God's glory.

Secular activities belong to the laity who by their expertise in various fields work with others in putting new projects in motion. Such persons have as their special role to bring the light of Christian wisdom to bear on life in the earthly city of man. In specific cases there is often no easily decernable solution which is uniquely Christian; no one should arrogate for himself the Church's endorsement of his opinion, but rather through honest discussion with others seek what is best for the general good of all. In all they do let them witness to Christ in human society.

For their part Church leaders are to so preach the Gospel that the laity will radiate its message in their earthly concerns. By the conduct of their lives in the midst of human affairs pastors will be the presence of the Church revealing Christ to the world. Above all let them work in a spirit of cooperation with all who serve the common welfare, and to achieve greater unity let them wipe out every trace of division by open dialogue. Sadly there have been and are among us those whose lives and actions do not accord with the Christian message. We exhort all to labor for a thorough reformation of their lives, so that in our work in the world the light of Christian experience may shine forth undimmed.

44. The Church has richly benefitted from the history of man's progress through the centuries. From earliest times she has learned to express Christ's truth by the help of ideas and in the culture of various peoples. And in this adaptation of her message to each nationality there has been a profitable exchange. Especially today when changes are so rapid, the Church relies on those versed in the many cultures of the world to help her pastors and theologians to relate the truths of the Gospel to the world all about us. The very sign of her unity, the Church's visible structure, is more suitably adjusted to our times when modern social developments are properly understood. Actually whoever promotes the human family is at the same time contributing to the Church insofar as she depends on external conditions for her well being.

45. In the totality of its interchange with the world, the Church as universal sacrament has but one intent: that God's kingdom may be fully established among men for their salvation. Now Jesus Christ is that perfect man who sums up all things in Himself: the goal of human history, its focal point and its center. United in His Spirit we the race of men journey toward the final summing up of human history in Christ: "the Alpha and the Omega, the First and the Last, the Beginning and the End" (Rv. 22:13).

PART II

46. We make the light of Christian principles our guide as we turn attention to certain

problems of special urgency for mankind: marriage and the family, culture, socio-economic life, politics, the community of nations and world peace.

CHAPTER I
The Dignity of Marriage and Family Life

47. A healthy marriage and a happy family life lie at the foundations not only of sound personal growth but of the whole structure of society as well. For Christians and indeed for all who deeply value marriage and the family, a growing respect for life and the fostering of all that unites couples and serves family stability are reasons for rejoicing. Yet such cherished hopes are being undermined by the evils of poligamy, divorce, and free love. Truly marriage and the family are seriously shaken when selfishness, impurity and contraception push many to a crisis of conscience. Nevertheless, because the sacred nature of marriage and family life deserve to be preserved and strengthened for the good of all humankind, we turn our attention to several key points of the Church's teaching for the clearer guidance of all who seriously work to strengthen these institutions.

48. The intimate partnership of life and love, which is marriage, deserves the name "covenant," not only because it comes about by the mutual promise of a freely consenting man and woman "until death," but because it is founded by the intention of the Creator of all that is good and holy for the human race. In expressing their free consent the

spouses take a marriage vow that accords with the God-given nature of this sacred bond. This point is really central, for on the stability of married life of man and woman depends the continuation of the race, the personal growth and final destiny of family members, and the dignity and peace of the whole family of man.

Although the highest glory of married love is the begetting and full nuturing of offspring, husband and wife in their marriage grow into more mature levels of self-giving, of seeing life through the needs of the other, and of generous sacrifice for the well-being of every family member. This can only happen where there exists a total bonding of love — genuine fidelity — between husband and wife who "are no longer two, but one flesh" (Mt. 19:6).

Like the covenant of old between God and His people, Christ the Lord, as the divine Lover of the Church, unites Christian couples through the sacred covenant of Matrimony, a sacrament and sign of Christ's love of His Church. Caught up in this mystery of God's love, the spouses are brought ever closer to Him and are strengthened for their duties as parents. They grow in the spirit of Christ and in the spirit of faith, hope, and charity for the glory of their Creator. And this growth in holiness involves the whole family, for children reflect the lives of faithful love of their father and mother who are the first heralds of the faith. Children contribute in their way to the happiness and holiness of their parents by responding to their love in the hardships of life and in the loneliness of advancing years. Thus the human family, firmly rooted in God, will manifest to all men the divine Savior's living presence in the world and the real beauty of the Church which is His spouse.

49. In both Scripture and secular literature the love between husband and wife is highly exalted; and rightly so, for as a deeply human experience, married love so refines the natural affection between two human persons that each seeks the good of the other and in spiritual friendship cherishes the other as another self. Two individuals become "we." In His desire to restore and elevate married life, Christ the Lord lavished the riches of His graces upon the love of husband and wife, even uniting it to His own divine love. Like Christ's love the love of the spouses is growing and creative, and like Christ's love expresses itself in giving, in sharing, in serving.

Through the acts proper to marriage, which are noble and honorable, spouses grow in love: a chaste union enriching both in joy and gratitude. This vital unity of heart and mind and will, excluding adultery, divorce and every inequality of the sexes, demands the greatest courage, the courage of faithful, truly generous hearts. Let spouses find in God, who is ever faithful, the source of their strength. As a glowing lamp, their way of life of perfect harmony, of fidelity to each other, and of devoted concern for the upbringing of their children will shine out as a witness to the total renewal of marriage and family life.

50. Love and marriage tend by nature itself to the procreation and education of

children, the supreme gift of married love. Let married couples then be collaborators in their God-given roles of transmitting human life and make this their own proper mission in life. With a truly human and Christian sense of responsibility, let couples form their judgments regarding the begetting of children in accord with God's own law. Although they do make their own decisions in this matter, they are to be docile and submissive to the Church's teaching office, which authentically interprets God's law in the light of the Gospel. This divine law reveals and enlightens the full meaning of married love and leads it to a truly human wholeness.

Procreation alone does not exhaust the value of married love. Even when there are no children despite the couple's earnest desire, the communion of love between the two continues to grow and retain its value as an unbreakable bond.

51. We realize that circumstances arising in the world of today may require that couples limit the number of offspring perhaps for a considerable time. Certainly this interruption of intimacy puts severe strains on the marriage and imperils their faithfulness to one another, not to mention the wholesome rearing of children. To solve these difficulties some actually propose murder in the forms of abortion or infanticide. The Church must emphasize again that there is no conflict between God's law for transmitting human life and the fostering of genuine married love. That vital mission of protecting life God has entrusted to human persons to be its

guardians. Once conceived, human life must be defended from all harm. And those acts of procreation so honored within the state of marriage must be ordered to accord with full human dignity. Consequently, when there is a question of harmonizing married love with the responsible transmitting of life, objective moral standards must be used which respect the full meaning of mutual self-giving and its natural issue in offspring. In this matter the faithful are not free to disregard the Church's sound teaching. Let them be convinced that the transmission of human life is to be evaluated not merely in terms of the present life, but most especially with reference to our eternal destiny.

52. As a school for human enrichment, family life must be characterized by harmony of minds and hearts especially in all that concerns the education of children. The father's active presence is as vital as is the loving care of the mother within the home. As children grow into responsible adulthood they should assume the choice of their vocation, including the option of Religious life. The choice should be theirs, free from pressures to marry or to choose a particular life partner. Ideally, the family includes the extended relationships spanning generations and these members enrich one another's lives by their care and service. And since the family is the foundation of society itself, community leaders by their influence should foster the welfare of the family, and public officials should promote the stability of domestic life among their citizens. Let all Christians give a constant witness to the

values of the family and cooperate with all who make these same values their own.

Those who are expert in scientific fields can do much for marriage and family life by their efforts to elaborate more thoroughly the various conditions which favor the proper regulation of births. Priests too by their special training and experience can be a strong force in sustaining and encouraging the people of God in their family roles. Finally let married people, conscious that they are created in the image of God and enjoy the dignity of children of God, strive within their exalted vocation to become witnesses of that love which Christ revealed to the world.

CHAPTER II

The Development of Culture

53. Human persons achieve a genuine sense of their humanity only through culture by which they set upon the goods of nature the imprint of their own values. By culture is meant all the ways human beings refine their spiritual and physical qualities touching their environment, social and civic life. So they express human experiences of the past, communicate them, and preserve them for posterity. Really one should speak of a rich variety of cultures, arising as they do from a diversity of life-styles, values, labor, self-expression, religion, laws, customs, science, and the arts.

54. So profound have been the changes in life today that we rightly speak of a new age of human history characterized by the

following: a highly critical judgment based on science; new insights into behavior from psychology; the view of an ever changing, developing world from historical studies; human customs that are more unified through community living; newly created mass cultures through communications that tie nations and societies together. The result is that a more universal form of culture is being fostered which yet preserves particular ways men express themselves in society.

55. A growing number of individuals in the various cultures are taking as their own the responsibility for fashioning the world of mankind toward a greater spiritual and moral maturity. What we see is the birth of a new humanism, a unity of all in truth and justice, and humanity defined by a common responsibility for mankind's life on this planet.

56. Despite the high hopes we feel for the progress of culture, a nice balance between many extremes must be kept. All, especially Christians, are called to maintain a harmony between an exchange among diverse cultures and keeping the character proper to each people; or the harmony between an expanding technology and a heritage of traditional values; or again between the specialist and the importance of a comprehensive outlook; and finally the harmony between a culture restricted to this earth with the other-world aspirations of mankind.

57. Their dedication to the Christian faith should encourage the faithful to a greater commitment for building a world that is more human. When a Christian strives

to make of his world a dwelling place more worthy of mankind, he realizes God's design that we perfect His creation, improve ourselves as persons, and serve our fellowmen. As such a person brings the human race to appreciate truth, goodness and beauty, he is a co-worker with his Creator; for by these endeavors, the human spirit is set free from material things to worship and contemplate the divine Lord of all things. Certainly there is danger that scientific progress can lead many to regard such methods of investigation as the final standard for all knowledge and produce an excessive confidence that man can know all things without the divine light. Yet such dangers do not outweigh the very positive value in modern cultural advances; such as, fidelity to truth, teamwork in technical matters, international cooperation, and responsibility for improving the lot of those who are deprived of cultural attainments. Cultivation of these values provides a preparation for the Gospel message of divine charity.

58. True to God's way of revealing Himself the Church has adapted herself to the various cultures of the centuries in order to proclaim and explain the message of Christ and to express it in worship and practice. True to her traditions, the Church is not tied to any one culture or form of expression regarding the Gospel message, for hers is a universal mission embracing peoples of all cultures. Because of this the Good News of Christ has been and continues to be as a yeast purifying, elevating, and enhancing every aspect of human cultures,

thus contributing to the growth of man's inner freedom.

59. We state clearly that the purpose of all cultural attainments is to serve an harmonious development of the human person and the common good of the human family. This means that culture must be allowed the freedom to make progress according to its own guidelines, with proper respect for individual and community rights. In line with past Councils we affirm this freedom of the arts and sciences to their own development. Thus every person has the right of pursuing truth and cultivating all human values. The proper role of governments is to assist in building up an environment for cultural expression, but in no way to bend culture to political purposes.

Christian Responsibility for Culture

60. Christians have the duty to urge those decisions by which governments assist all to acquire the benefits of a cultural life in keeping with human dignity. A start would be to ensure for all the ability to read and to write. Then by every means there should be provided the chance for higher education for all whose talents suit them for a fuller development of cultural attainment. At the same time any condition of life that forms a barrier to people's cultural advancement, such as among rural dwellers or working class folk, should be corrected. Certainly the

status of women should be so enhanced that they too fully share in the building of human culture.

61. It is the Christian, and hence the human, view that the more a person grows in a diversity of cultural interests the more a total person he becomes, for he blends the values of mind and heart and spirit into a unity. If this training is well begun in the bosom of the family, the young person readily makes use of the abounding resources now spread out before him. Among these the boom in book publishing and the mass media can be cited, coupled with a greater amount of leisure time for recreation, study, tourism, and sports. Although it is true that all of these foster a better sense of unity among the family of mankind and deserve the fullest support of all, yet these opportunities will remain barren unless people fully appreciate the meaning of cultural progress and above all what makes up genuine progress in culture.

62. New discoveries in science, history and philosophy have a way of posing new problems for the person of faith. But this leads Christian teachers to give an account of the faith in terms that are better understood in modern times. And so the doctrines of faith, which must remain true to their essential meaning, need to be expressed in the light of modern psychology and sociology; and thus lead all to a life of faith that is more mature. Literature and art, expressing as they do man's deeper experience of himself in this world, powerfully contribute to ennobling humanity. We ought to provide a greater scope of free expression for artists

and invite them to enhance the worship of God through lofty creations, with all respect for the diversity of ethnic cultures.

Once Christians appreciate the newer ways of thinking and feeling of modern culture, they can with a greater sense of balance lead their lives in full accord with their own traditional values. Finally, we urge a closer collaboration among scholars in every field and especially urge theologians to become ever more competent teachers in ways that gain the respect of persons in diverse fields. We call for a more thorough study of theology on the part of lay people. We want all, clerical and lay, to exercise their studies of the faith in a lawful air of freedom, tempered by humility and courage.

CHAPTER III
Economic and Social Life

63. The one aim and focus of all economic activity and social life is the welfare of the human person and the society of which he is part. At present there is in the world an ever growing efficiency in meeting the material needs of the human family. But certain factors cause great concern: a mentality that our lives are governed by economic forces alone; a vast disparity between rich and poor, between abundance and misery. Add to this that many cannot exercise any responsibility over their living conditions. These situations tend to divide peoples and nations to the point of endangering world peace. Men of our time want to resolve these problems by a better use of technology and resources

as well as by a change of attitudes. We, for our part, recalling the principles of justice which the Church has worked out, will offer these as guidelines for a fairer development and distribution of the goods of the earth.

64. Certainly, in view of the growing populations of the earth, there must be an expansion of technical progress and a more creative enterprise in the production of goods of all kinds. Yet all such progress must be funneled into the service of mankind — the total needs of human persons throughout the world regardless of social status, race or national origin. Only in this way can God's will for the human race be fulfilled.

65. Since the benefits of economic progress are for peoples in all nations, all should have a voice in the direction of this development of the goods of the earth. Efforts of those in the private sector should be coordinated with decisions taken by governments; and these should not assume all rights for the collective good. Nor should the notion of individual freedom stifle the efforts for the common good of all. Rather, all citizens have the right and the duty to foster the material advances of their country, and are wrong if they retard progress by hoarding up as their own resources needed for the benefit of all.

66. Justice demands that there be an end to the vast economic differences existing in the world. An important area for improvement is in agriculture through better production and marketing. This can come about where farmers use modern methods for increased productivity. Workers who migrate to other countries should be treated with

fairness both in wages and working conditions. Host countries should treat such migrants as persons with human dignity: workers who support their families in decent housing and with equal opportunities with other citizens. As industry turns more and more to automation, the long-range employment and security of workers should be maintained through technical training programs.

Guidelines for Economic and Social Living

67. Human labor remains the superior element in the economic enterprise, for through it man exerts his dominion over the material world for the building up of his own human dignity. Nor is it a mere means to material well-being, for through labor humanity is joined with Jesus Christ in His divine work of reconciling the world with His Father. Societies have the obligation to provide opportunities for their citizens to be employed, earn a livelihood for themselves and their families in keeping with their human dignity, and contribute to the good of their country. Those economic systems which exploit human labor on whatever pretext are intollerable and unjust. Rather, the system, any system, should serve the needs of persons: material needs, cultural, social and religious activities, as well as needed rest and leisure time.

68. The organization of commercial life demands the best efforts of all concerned — owners, employers, management and employees. Decisions in these matters should be

made by institutions on a higher level than just the business itself, and workers should have a part to play since their welfare depends on such decisions. Speaking of the rights of workers, we affirm their right to associations which represent them, and expect that through them workers will expand their responsible role in the common goals of the economy. In the event of disputes between economic groups, peaceful solutions through honest discussion is the aim. Yet the workers' right to strike must be safeguarded as a necessary means for their protection when their rights are threatened.

69. By the divine plan the goods of the earth are destined for the use of all mankind and to be shared by the human family in accord with justice and charity. Those who own property must regard it as having benefit for others also, and they are bound to share their goods for the help of the needy to the extent of their ability. Where the private property system is not the custom, other methods of guaranteeing to each the necessities of life are in force. Where such customs do not meet modern needs, let them yield to prudent modification. Other countries use methods of social insurance and security to provide for their citizens in times of want and for old age; but let such methods not lull people into a state of passive irresponsibility and laziness.

70. Investments ought to be aimed at providing employment and keeping income stable. The really serious responsibility here is to keep a happy balance between the needs for decent living for citizens in the present

time and the requirements of capital for future generations of citizens. Fiscal decisions should be made with an eye to keeping one's own country sound as well as being accountable for the needs of others, especially of underdeveloped nations.

71. The human person for the proper flowering of his freedom within a social context must have the chance to own property for his own use and disposal. This right might be exercised in many ways, such as through programs of social security, social service benefits, and the possession of professional skills. Since human beings find their proper growth in the context of society, it stands to reason that society can and must regulate the individual use and even ownership of property, but always in accord with equitable norms. Thus governments may transfer ownership to public use for the common good of the citizens of the state, providing just compensation to the owners.

In some economically deprived areas, urgent reforms are called for to remedy conditions in which human beings on a large scale live as serfs to great landowners, while vast land areas lie unproductive. The state in such situations has the duty to take action; let land reform begin by dividing up shares for those able to make it productive; let employment tactics be used to provide a secure income for all; let the needed resources be set up: equipment, training, and organizations for cooperation. In all such programs compensation according to justice should be made wherever land is expropriated from rightful owners.

72. We heartily encourage those Christian people who work for a social order based on justice and charity, and urge them to greater loyalty to the Gospel of Christ which is expressed in the spirit of the Beatitudes. As they seek first the Kingdom of God, they will express toward their fellowmen a stronger and purer love.

CHAPTER IV
The Political Community

73. Among the changes in political life of peoples, we cite as noteworthy the insistence that human rights be protected in civil society: the rights of assembly, free expression, and religious practice. And from the secure base of protected rights flows the growing concern that responsibilities for all aspects of civil life be shouldered by all citizens, be they minorities in race, religion, ethnic origin or social status. Contrary to closed and oppressive political systems, that political life is more truly human which encourages a sense of justice, goodwill and service to the common good.

74. The funadmental reason for the political community is just this: what citizens as individuals and groups cannot achieve on their own for the common advantage of all of their society, that they can promote by forming a political organization aimed at a fuller human life for all. Because men differ on what specific means are required for this, it is natural that political authority exist, so that the efforts of all by a moral force be directed to the common good (which embraces

the sum-total of all those conditions of social life which enable all to achieve efficacious fulfillment) in freedom and responsibility. Citizens are free to choose their form of government and decide on the appointment of those who exercise this authority. Thus rulers of the State have the duty within the limits of morality to advance progressively the common good of all; citizens are bound in conscience to obey them. When rulers overstep their authority to the point of oppression of citizens' rights, citizens, while carrying out all that is for the common welfare, still may legitimately defend their own rights within the limits of God's law. Though the forms of political authority may vary greatly according to cultural backgrounds of peoples, the aim must ever be the same; the formation of peace-loving people ready in the service of their fellowmen.

75. It is well that states encourage their citizens without discrimination to play active roles in improving their governments, serving in public office, and exercising their right to vote. To facilitate citizen cooperation and responsibility, there must exist a system of laws providing for a separation of powers of government and for the protection of civil rights. Law should indicate citizen duties, such as, that of rendering service for the good of the nation. The State should promote private associations of citizens and allow them to carry on their activities independently without excessive reliance on public authority to make demands and impose controls. Though public authority must intervene in citizen affairs to make it possible for individ-

uals and groups to function effectively, still to preserve individual freedom and progress as well, such intervention must be prudent and restrained, and used only when necessary. But totalitarian methods which violate human and civil rights are a degradation of humanity.

Citizens should be generous and loyal to their country, but keep a more basic loyalty to the human family. Christians by their respect for the rights and opinions of others should be models of a dedication to the common good, of responsible freedom, and of the blend of unity within fruitful diversity. Political parties should put the common good of all before all partisan interests. We issue a serious call for a thorough civil and political education for the young and a call for those having talent for political activity to come forward to serve their fellowmen in the building up of true justice in their communities.

76. The relationship between the State and the Church needs clarification by distinguishing their respective roles in human life. The Church is not identified with any political system. She is the sign and safeguard of that aspect of human life that is beyond this world. And though independent of one another, the State and the Church can serve the human community better, the better both cooperate together. Since man's destiny extends beyond the temporal order and human history, the Church's role is to teach mankind the Gospel leading to eternal salvation. Through this teaching men are drawn to practice justice and charity toward all through the exercise of freedom and responsibility within a political order. Church leaders, true

to the example of the Apostles, carry on the task of proclaiming the Gospel in reliance on the power of God and on means that are proper to the Gospel message. Because of the close union between this world and the Kingdom of God, the Church uses temporal things in her work. And though she is willing to renounce privileges and the exercise of certain rights to insure her witness role, she claims at all times and places her freedom to proclaim her teachings about man and society and her judgments on moral matters even when these touch on political and economic matters. The means she may use are those in accord with the Gospel and aimed at the salvation of the human person and the elevation of all that is true and good in human life.

CHAPTER V
Keeping Peace Through the International Community

77. The constant threat of global warfare is the supreme crisis for the human race in its march toward maturity. There simply will be no really human world unless all people sincerely devote themselves to the cause of peace among men and nations. Against this backdrop we now address the problems of peace and of war and of world cooperation in securing peace based on justice and charity.

78. More than just the absence of war, peace is the fruit of that just ordering of human society which brings about the common

good of the whole human family. Because of the weakness of mankind, a continually renewed effort is demanded for the achieving of peace among men. For this reason there must be a firm determination on the part of all to respect the dignity of one another, to deal together in trust, and above all to practice an abiding fraternal love. As such love stems basically from the reconciling work of Christ, Christians are to be in the forefront working for peace through cooperation with peace-loving peoples. We praise those who renounce violence in their desire to vanquish sin—the root of hate and conflict—by their practice of charity.

79. Savagery is the proper word for modern warfare carried on as it is with the weaponry, subversion, and terrorist tactics that threaten such barbarities as the world has not seen till now. Recoiling from such infamy as genocide, the conscience of mankind rises up to assert the moral force of the natural law of peoples of the earth. Let no one offer the excuse for such crimes that he was carrying out orders from higher authority. Courageous indeed are those who stand against such a perversion of authority.

The various international treaties which are designed to curb the savagery of war need to be preserved and improved to meet modern needs. Some legal standing should be given to those who in conscience refuse to bear arms. Realistically, in the absence of international authority with real competence states retain the right of self-defense even to the last resort of war. Yet the fact that national leaders are responsible for the interests of their citizens does not justify military force to impose domination on others nor to use indiscriminate methods of war. We point out, however, that dutiful military personnel are loyally serving the security and freedom of their fellow countrymen.

80. Look for a moment at the immense havoc of war now possible due to modern weapons: superpowers are capable of the complete slaughter of one another and of devastating aftereffects for the rest of the globe. The very future of the human race depends upon the decisions which men of this generation make with respect to total war. This then is our solemn declaration: warlike acts which are directed to the indiscriminate destruction of cities and areas with their inhabitants merit unequivocal condemnation. Considering the possibilities of escalation of hostilities to the hazard of the human race, we implore all leaders of states to consider before God and men their fateful responsibility.

81. Several nations have chosen to increase their stockpile of weapons as a retaliation and deterrent to potential foes. This is their option for keeping the peace. Yet this arms race with its balance of power is no guarantee of peaceful relations. The vast expense of armaments render impossible the alleviation of human misery, thus preventing nations from eleminating the causes of war. Furthermore this option, since it merely incites a spreading danger of war, must be rejected as one of the great curses of the human race. Let us take our warning from past catastrophes of which the arms race is a pre-

lude, and find in due time ways of resolving conflicts among nations that befit human dignity.

82. The aim is clear: a time when all war is outlawed by international agreement. The essential requirement is also clear: the formation of a universally acknowledged truly international authority with power to keep all nations secure under a rule of just laws. Until this is achieved, there is much to be done. First, using present international bodies men should renounce the enslaving fear of the arms race and replace it with the yeast of mutual trust. Then a full scale disarmament bound by treaties and guarantees can begin. Next, active support should be given to all those leaders who labor at the demanding task of building peace and goodwill among men and nations; they are in the vanguard of that spirit of international respect for all which is the hallmark of human maturity. Further, many meetings among nations resulting in concrete agreements deserve the active support of public opinion within the various nations involved. Finally, to lay to rest every kind of contempt, discord and mistrust among men, an education that is truly international is called for, especially that education which reaches the hearts of men and there effects a change to aspirations for peace.

Unless the hearts and mentality of humankind yields to sentiments of trust and peace, there will be no humankind left on this planet. The Church has not lost hope, however, and with the Apostle calls out to the world: "Now is the day of salvation" (2 Cor. 6:2).

The International Community

83. What cause strife, violence and war between nations and mankind? Surely injustice in first place; also unchecked economic disparities existing between nations. Such causes can be overcome only by a resolute coordination of efforts on the international level.

84. The world-wide community of nations needs to organize itself for the common welfare of all mankind, with special agencies to meet the more pressing needs of the world's population: food, health and education, especially among developing nations, refugees, and migrants. We enthusiastically support already existing organizations at the international level which are working out the most serious problems of our time, such as the prevention of wars and the alleviation of human misery.

85. Peoples who have gained political independence need international collaboration to give them economic stability. This means that the material resources and professional training of the citizens of many developing countries must come from abroad. Such aid as grants, loans and investments, although given in generosity and accepted with full honesty, will fail unless there are profound changes in present world trade policies. We look for men to set aside greed, self-seeking and rivalry, and in their place find a common ground for establishing a worldwide order of commerce based on justice for all.

86. Serious consideration should be given to these norms for cooperation: a) De-

veloping nations should know that real progress comes through the efforts and work of their own citizens elaborating native resources and their own culture. b) Affluent nations need to educate themselves to their task of helping poorer nations achieve a more stable economy within their own borders, so that they may gain greater self-sufficiency. c) An international organization of nations needs to coordinate all efforts to the end that there is a fair distribution of resources of the earth. Let it regulate international commerce according to justice so that less developed countries are provided with adequate means to achieve economic success.

87. To meet the very serious problem of rapidly increasing population in many lands, the full cooperation of the international community is demanded. In particular technical advances in agriculture need to be shared with the entire world coupled with a fairer distribution of land ownership. Within each nation let experts recommend solutions to the population problem which fall within the scope of governmental rights and duties. We urge all to see that solutions offered to check population growth accord well with the moral law and respect the right of persons to marry and bear offspring. So that parents can acquire a true human sense of responsibility in this matter a careful moral and religious formation is called for. Information about moral and valid methods of birth regulation should be made available.

88. Christians especially should be conspicuous in the ways of fostering brotherhood among all peoples. What a scandal to see

so-called Christian nations abounding in the goods of the earth while millions suffer want and misery! Surely Christ through them calls for the charity of those who profess to follow the poor Man of Nazareth. Volunteers who serve people in nations other than their own are a praiseworthy example reminding us of the duty we have to give to those who need, and to give even when it hurts. Let there be a genuine collaboration with all persons of generosity in contributing to the needy of the world; such is the response our charity calls for.

89. The Church is unremitting in her efforts for peace and brotherly union among peoples. She is clearly present in the community of nations as a strong moral force stimulating the cooperation of all and urging the responsibilities we all have to serve the cause of human solidarity everywhere.

90. Already several Catholic international associations are making a vital contribution to world justice and peace. They should be strengthened and supported, and work in concert with other Christians to promote a sense of universality. We suggest that to this end the universal Church sponsor a special office devoted to justice and peace throughout the world.

The Conclusion

91-93. The teachings we have presented are sincerely offered to help all men of good will to become more aware of their destiny and their dignity, and to strive for a true brotherhood in genuine love. Standing as a sign of this brotherhood and eager to serve all humanity, the Church invites all to sincere dialogue in the quest for peace among men and for the discovery of truth. Even though differences of worship and belief separate us, common human values bind us together; let there be unity in what is necessary, freedom in what is doubtful, and charity in everything.

Dogmatic Constitution on Divine Revelation

(*Dei Verbum,* November 18, 1965)

A paraphrase by
Rev. E. J. Jacques, S.J.

Preface

1. United in Council we listen to the Word of God and proclaim it faithfully. In accord with the Councils of Trent and Vatican I, we want to teach about divine revelation and about how it comes down to the present.

CHAPTER I

2. God wished to reveal Himself and His plan of salvation. His plan is that men might go to the Father through Christ and in the Holy Spirit and become sharers in the divine nature. By this revelation God speaks to men as friends, lives among them, and welcomes them to fellowship with Him. This plan of revelation comes about through words and deeds. The deeds show and confirm the teachings. The words proclaim the deeds and clarify the plan intrinsic to them. The deepest truth about God and the salvation of men shines forth in Christ. He is at once the medium of revelation and the whole fullness of it.

3. Since God through Christ is the Creator and Preserver of all things, they point to Him. He wished to clear the way to salvation, so He revealed Himself from the beginning to our first parents. After their fall He gave them the hope of salvation and cared endlessly for men. This way He gave eternal life to all who looked for salvation by doing good. He called Abraham, the Patriarchs, then sent Moses and the prophets to His people to teach them to recognize Him as the only living and true God and to wait for the promised Savior.

4. Finally God spoke to us in His Son. He sent His Son, the eternal Word of God, Jesus Christ. He was to live among men and speak to them about the hidden things of God. He was to do the work of salvation His Father had given Him to do. Thus by His presence and by all He did Jesus completed revelation. He certified that God is with us to free us from sin and death and to raise us to eternal life.

The Christian plan then as the new and final covenant will never pass away. There is to be no further public revelation until Christ comes again.

5. Man's response to God's revelation is to commit his whole self freely to God. He does this by offering the complete service of his mind and will to God's revelation. This faith must be helped by the grace of God and the work of the Holy Spirit. The Holy Spirit turns the heart to God, opens the eyes of the mind, and gives to all joy in believing. The Holy Spirit also completes faith and brings about a deeper understanding of revelation.

6. God wished to reveal Himself and His plan for salvation to share with men the divine goodness which man could not even know about.

The Council teaches that men could know God as the beginning and end of all things from a study of creation. But God also reveals things that man could know from his own unaided inquiries.

CHAPTER II

7. What God revealed for the salvation of all He made sure would be handed on complete to all generations. Christ, the fullness of

revelation, commissioned the Apostles to preach the Gospel to all. This Gospel was promised through the prophets, fulfilled and promulgated by Christ, and is the source of all saving truth and moral instruction.

This message of salvation was written down by the Apostles or by apostolic men. By their preaching, example, and orders the Apostles handed on what they had learned from Christ's words, deeds, and life and from the inspiration of the Holy Spirit. To keep the Gospel whole and alive in the Church the Apostles left bishops as their successors. The Apostles gave the bishops their own duty as teachers. This Tradition and the Bible are now like a mirror in which the Church gazes at God until the time when God grants a face-to-face vision.

8. With unbroken succession the apostolic preaching, contained in a special way in the inspired books, must go on until the end of time. So the Apostles warn the faithful to hold to what they have received. This is what the Apostles themselves have received and hand on. It concerns living a holy life and increasing the faith of the People of God. The Church in her theology, life and worship continues and hands on all that she is, all that she believes.

This apostolic Tradition flourishes in the Church with the aid of the Holy Spirit. Through the prayer and fervor of believers and the preaching of bishops the understanding of what has been handed on grows. The Church is always heading toward the goal of divine truth when the words of God will be fully realized in her.

The witnesses to this Tradition are the Fathers of the Church. Their writings are used in the prayer-life of the faithful. The complete list (canon) of the books of the Bible is known through Tradition. Through Tradition the Bible is more thoroughly understood and put into practice. God, who spoke long ago to Israel, continues His conversation in this way with the bride of His Son. Through the Holy Spirit the living voice of the Gospel speaks to the Church and to the world through the Church. The Holy Spirit brings all truth to believers and makes the words of Christ richly alive in them.

9. Tradition and the Bible are closely interconnected. Both come from the same origin, join together, and aim at the same goal. The Bible is the message of God put in writing under the inspiration of the Holy Spirit. Tradition delivers the word of God which was entrusted by Christ and the Holy Spirit to the Apostles and their successors. They by their preaching preserve, explain and spread the Word of God. Thus the Church does not draw certitude about all of revelation from the Bible alone. So both Tradition and the Bible are to be accepted in the same way.

10. Tradition and the Bible form one deposit in the Church of the Word of God. This is handed on through the union of bishops and believers. They are united in the faith of the Apostles, in the life of the Church, in the Eucharist, and in prayer.

Only the living magisterium of the Church (teaching office of the Church) has been given the duty of interpretation of the Word of God which is found in the Bible or in Tradition. This magisterium is not over the Word of God but serves it. The magisterium teaches only the Word of God it has received. It listens to the Word of God, guards it, and explains it. Everything that is proposed to be believed as divinely revealed comes from this one deposit of faith.

By God's wise design Tradition, the Bible and the Church's magisterium cannot exist without one another since they are so interconnected. Through the Holy Spirit, all three together, each in its own way, bring about the salvation of souls.

CHAPTER III

11. The Holy Spirit inspired the writing of what has been revealed in the Bible. Inasmuch as the Bible was written under the inspiration of the Holy Spirit, God is the author of it and as such it was entrusted to the Church. God uses men, who use their own faculties and powers in writing the Bible. They are true authors but they recorded all and only what God wanted recorded.

What the inspired authors assert is asserted by the Holy Spirit. Therefore it must be said that the Bible teaches firmly, faithfully, and without error the truth which God wanted in it for our salvation.

12. God speaks to men in the Bible, through men, and in a human way. The interpreter of the Bible must search out what the writers really intended and what God wanted to reveal through their words.

Among other things the literary form must be examined. Truth varies in its expression depending on whether it is in history or in prophecy or in poetry or in other types of writing. The interpreter must seek the sense of the writer according to his times and the level of his culture. So he must investigate the usual types of writing in the time of each writer.

But the whole of the Bible must also be kept in mind. It was written through the Holy Spirit through whom it must also be read and interpreted. Anything about the interpretation of the Bible is subject to the final judgment of the Church.

13. In the Bible God's marvelous condescension is revealed. Just as the Word of God took on human flesh, so the words of God in the Bible are expressed in human language.

CHAPTER IV

14. God prepared the salvation of all by choosing a people for Himself. God revealed Himself to Israel as the only living and true God through His words and deeds. Israel was to transmit this to all people. The plan of salvation is shown in the Old Testament. Therefore these inspired books have a permanent value.

15. The plan in the Old Testament was especially to prepare for the coming of the Messiah. The Old Testament reveals knowledge of God and of man and the ways God deals with man. These books contain some imperfect and temporary things but show how God educates His people. These books contain teachings, wisdom and prayers, and must be reverently used by the faithful.

16. God is the inspirer and author of both Testaments. He hid the New in the Old and makes the Old shine forth in the New. Christ made a New Covenant in His blood. The Old Testament gets its full meaning from the New Testament and also helps explain it.

CHAPTER V

17. The word of God is the power of God for the salvation of all believers. This shines forth most forcefully in the New Testament. When the time came, the Word became flesh and lived among us. Christ began the Kingdom of God on earth. He revealed the Father and Himself by His words and deeds. He finished His work by His death, resurrection, ascension, and sending of the Holy Spirit. He alone has the words of eternal life and draws all to Himself when He has been raised from the earth.

The Apostles were to preach the Gospel, inspire faith in Jesus, Christ and Lord, and to gather together the Church. So to the Apostles the mystery of Christ was revealed as to no one else. The New Testament gives witness about these things.

18. The Gospels especially excel because they give witness about the life and teaching of our Savior. The Church always and everywhere holds that the four Gospels have an apostolic origin. The Gospels of Matthew, Mark, Luke, and John reflect what the Apostles preached at Christ's command.

19. The Church teaches that the four Gospels historically relate what Jesus did and taught for man's salvation. After the ascension the Apostles enlightened by the

Holy Spirit preached with a fuller understanding what Jesus did and taught. The evangelists wrote a kind of synthesis of what they received from the Apostles. The evangelists kept the form of preaching and explained the truth about Jesus to the Church of their times. They wrote to give us the truth from their own experience or from the witness of those who were with Jesus.

20. Besides the four Gospels the canon of the New Testament contains the letters of Paul and other inspired apostolic writings. These explain more and more the teaching of Christ, preach the saving power of His work, and announce His glorious return.

The Lord Jesus was with His Apostles as He promised and He sent the Holy Spirit to them to lead them into the fullness of truth.

CHAPTER VI

21. In the liturgy above all the Church receives the bread of life from the table of the Word of God and of the Body of Christ and gives it to the faithful. Therefore the Church has always venerated the Bible as the Body of the Lord has been venerated. The supreme rule of faith has always been these two: the Bible and Tradition. The Bible gives us the Word of God put into inspired writings and makes the voice of the Holy Spirit heard in the words of the Apostles and prophets. Both preaching and the Christian religion are sustained and ruled by the Bible. In the Bible the Heavenly Father meets His children with great love and speaks to them. The force and power of

the word of God is the support and strength of the Church. The Bible is the spiritual food for the Church.

22. The Bible should be accessible to all the faithful. The Church at the beginning received the Greek translation of the Hebrew Old Testament as her own. Other translations were always held in honor. The Church provides for translations. Translations can be done in cooperation with the separated Christians.

23. The Church yearns to go forward each day in understanding the Bible. The Church encourages the study of the Fathers of the Church and of the liturgy. Catholic biblical interpreters and theologians should use the aids that help the People of God to reach the true purpose of the Bible.

We encourage biblical scholars to continue the good work they have begun.

24. The foundation of theology is the written Word of God and Tradition. Theology is renewed by contact with the Word of God and seeks with faith all truth in the mystery of Christ. The Bible contains the Word of God, and because it is inspired it truly is the Word of God. So biblical studies are the soul of theology. All ministry of the word in the Church derives benefit from the Bible.

25. All clerics must study the Bible. We also urge all the faithful to read the Bible. Prayer should accompany the reading of the Bible.

Bishops should give instruction about the right use of the Bible and make proper translations available.

Translations with necessary explanations should be made available even to non-Christians.

26. Reading the Bible fills the heart more and more with the treasure of revelation given to the Church. Just as the life of the Church increases through frequent Communion, it will also increase through use of the Bible.

Dogmatic Constitution on the Church

(Lumen Gentium, November 21, 1964)

A paraphrase by
Marina E. Ruffolo

CHAPTER I
The Mystery of the Church

1. Christ is the saving light for the nations. United in Council we desire to shed on all mankind this light already radiant in the Church, a light which she proclaims through the Gospel. The Church is like a sacrament or a sign of our union with God and an instrument of the unity of the whole human race. Because of this we intend to speak about the nature and the universal mission of the Church. Present conditions make this aspect of the Church more urgent.

Through social, technical and cultural bonds men are becoming more closely joined together. It is through the Church that they can reach full unity in Christ.

2. The Eternal Father created all things and gave man the destiny of sharing His divine life. Even after man's fall in Adam God, looking forward to Christ, did not abandon man. He decided to gather into the Church all who believe in Christ. The Church has been foretold from the beginning of the world, prepared for in the history of Israel and its covenant, revealed in Christ, manifested by the outpouring of the Spirit, and will be gloriously completed at the end of time. Then all the just will be gathered together in the universal Church in the Father's house.

3. The Son came, sent from the Father. In the Son the Father chose us and destined us to be His adopted children. He wanted to restore all things to Himself through the Son. Christ, then, began the kingdom of

heaven on earth. He revealed the mystery of who He is. He redeemed us by His obedience. The Church, the Kingdom of Christ already here as a sign, visibly grows in the world through the power of God. As often as the sacrifice of the cross is celebrated at the altar, the work of our redemption is brought about. At the same time the Eucharistic Bread represents and brings about the unity of believers. The faithful make up one body in Christ. All men are called to this union with Christ from whom we have come, by whom we live and to whom we are en route.

4. Christ accomplished the work His Father gave Him to do on earth. Then He sent the Holy Spirit on Pentecost to sanctify the Church and to give those who believe in Christ access to the Father through the Spirit. He is the Spirit of life. Through this Spirit the Father gives life to men dead through sin and will raise their mortal bodies in the power of Christ. The Spirit lives in the Church and in the hearts of the faithful as in a temple. He prays and gives witness of their adoption as God's children. The Spirit leads the Church into truth. The Spirit instructs and directs the Church by various gifts. Through the power of the Gospel He makes the Church ever young and constantly renews her and leads her to her goal. Thus the whole Church appears as a people made one with the unity of the Father and of the Son and of the Holy Spirit.

5. The mystery of the Church was shown at its beginning. For Jesus began His Church by preaching the good news: the coming of the

Kingdom of God promised in the Old Testament. This kingdom shone before men in the word, works, and presence of Christ. The word of the Lord is like a seed which is planted through faith and then grows by its own power until harvest. The miracles of Jesus prove the kingdom has come to earth. Above all, the kingdom is shown in the person of Christ who is the Son of God and the Son of man. He has come to serve and to give His life as a ransom for the many.

After His sufferings and death Jesus rose as Lord, Messiah, and Eternal Priest. He sent the promised Spirit from the Father to His disciples. So the Church has been given gifts by Christ and faithfully keeps His commands of charity, humility, and abnegation. The Church has received the mission of telling about the Kingdom of Christ and God, of setting it up everywhere. The Church is the seed and the beginning of this kingdom on earth. The Church grows and yearns for the perfect kingdom and hopes to be joined gloriously with the King.

6. There are many images for the kingdom in the Old Testament. These give us some insight into the nature of the Church. The various areas of human life used as images are: the work of shepherds, farmers, builders, and family and married life.

The Church is a sheepfold, Christ is the gate. The Church is a flock, God is the shepherd.

The Church is the field of God. Israel is an old olive tree in that field. Or the true vine is Christ and the branches are the members of the Church.

The Church is the house of God. Christ is the cornerstone. The Apostles build on that foundation. The Church is a holy temple or the new Jerusalem built of living stones.

The Church is a mother, a spouse for the Lamb. These are images of the pilgrim Church on earth. Her true life is with Christ in God.

7. By His death and resurrection the Son of God in His human nature overcame death. He redeemed man. He transformed man into a new creation. By the giving of His Spirit He made His brothers into His Mystical Body.

In that Body the life of Christ is spread to the faithful. In a hidden and real way they are united to the sufferings and glorification of Christ through the sacraments. Through Baptism we are conformed to Christ. In the rite the union with Christ's death is represented and brought about. In the Eucharist we really share in the Body of the Lord. We are raised to communion with Him and among ourselves. We all become members of His Body.

In a human body many members form one body. So do the faithful in Christ. There is also a diversity of members and duties in the building up of the Body of Christ. One Spirit gives His various gifts for the needs of the Church. One gift that stands out is the grace of Apostles. The Spirit has placed these gifts or charisms under their authority. The Spirit produces and urges charity among the faithful. If one member suffers, all suffer; if one member is honored, all are honored.

The head of the Body is Christ. All members should be conformed to Him. We follow in the footsteps of His sufferings to be glorified with Him.

We help one another to salvation through His power in His Body which is the Church.

To bring all this about He gives us His Spirit which is like the soul in a human body. Christ loves the Church as His bride and adorns it with His divine gifts.

8. Christ, the only Mediator, set up and continuously maintains the Church, the visible community of faith, hope, and charity. From it truth and grace are spread to all. The Church is at the same time both a hierarchical organization and the Mystical Body of Christ, the Church on earth and the Church blessed with heavenly riches. But there is only one reality, in which there are human and divine parts. This mystery is like the mystery of the Incarnate Word. The human nature of the Divine Word is forever united to Him and serves as the visible means of salvation. The social structure of the Church likewise serves the growth of the Body of Christ through the Spirit.

There is only one holy, catholic, and apostolic Church. Our Savior handed it over to Peter to shepherd. He and the other Apostles were commissioned to spread it and rule over it. This Church subsists in the Catholic Church governed by the successor of Peter and the bishops in communion with him. There are many traces of holiness and truth outside this Church. These gifts tend toward Catholic unity.

The Church is called to the same path as Christ. He worked redemption in poverty and persecution. The Church communicates redemption in the same way. The Church uses human resources, not for earthly glory, but to spread humility and abnegation by its own example. The Church serves Christ by finding His image in the poor and suffering and by surrounding them with love. Christ was without sin but came to atone for sin. The Church takes in sinners and lives a life of continuous penance and renewal by being both holy yet always in need of purification.

The Church announces the death of the Lord until He comes (1 Cor. 11:26). Her pilgrimage takes place through persecution in the world and consolations from God. The Church is strengthened by the power of the risen Lord. By this power the internal and external difficulties are overcome with patience and love. Now in shadow, but faithfully, the Church reveals Christ's mystery. Finally it will be apparent in clear light.

CHAPTER II
The People of God

9. Through the ages God has always graced those who have loved Him and sought to do right. However, God intended to save mankind not individually, but in a people who would love and serve Him; so He chose the Israelites and with them made an alliance or covenant. Slowly through the ages He made known to them His plans for the new and everlasting alliance (New Testament). This came about through the coming of Christ, the Word of God made man, who brought us the full revelation of the message

of salvation. Christ instituted this alliance, calling together Jews and non-Jews, who were to become one, not according to the flesh, but in the Spirit. This race would be the "new" People of God. So, through Baptism, reborn spiritually from an incorruptible seed, we are finally established as "a chosen race, a royal priesthood...the People he claims for his own" (1 Pt. 2:9-10). Our head in God is Christ. Our state is that of dignity and freedom of sons of God in whose hearts the Holy Spirit dwells as in a temple. Our law is the "new" commandment to love as Christ loved us. Our destiny is the Kingdom of God.

We truly represent a most sure seed of unity, hope and salvation for the whole human race. As the new People of God, we are Christ's instruments for the redemption of the whole world.

All those who believe in Christ, God has gathered and established as the "Church" that it may be a visible sign and sacrament of this saving unity. The Church, destined to extend to all regions of the earth, enters into man's history reaching beyond all limits of time and peoples. Advancing through trials and tribulations, the Church is strengthened by God's grace and led by the Holy Spirit until, through bearing the cross with her Lord, she arrives at that Light which knows no setting.

10. Christ, by our rebirth in the Spirit (Baptism), consecrated us as a holy priesthood to God. The "common" priesthood of lay people differs from the "ministerial" priesthood of the clergy in an essential way. The ministerial priest, by the sacred powers he

has, shepherds the priestly people who are the laity; in Christ's place he offers the Eucharistic Sacrifice of the Mass in the name of all of us. We, by virtue of our common priesthood, participate in the offering of the Eucharist and enter into worship of God by receiving the sacraments.

11. Our unity as a priestly people is brought into operation through the divine act of the sacraments. Through Baptism we are incorporated into the Church and reborn as sons of God. We become Christians with the obligation to profess before men the faith we receive from God through the Church. Bound more intimately to the Church by Confirmation, we are endowed with special strength from the Holy Spirit and are more strictly obliged to spread and defend the faith. Taking part in the Eucharistic Sacrifice which is the fount and summit of the whole Christian life, we offer the divine Victim to God and offer ourselves along with Him, manifesting our unity in Christ and one another. The Sacrament of Penance reconciles us to God by obtaining pardon for the sins committed against Him. By the anointing with oil and the prayers of the priests, the whole Church prays for the sick. Those in Holy Orders (clergy) are appointed in Christ's name to shepherd the People of God. In the Sacrament of Matrimony Christian married couples help one another to attain holiness in their married life and in the rearing of their children. Through the special graces of this state of life they continue through the centuries the People of God. The family is like the domestic Church; the parents, by

word, deed and example, are the first heralds of the faith for their children. In family life there is nurtured the seed of religious vocations. Whatever our condition or state, we are all called by God to perfect holiness.

12. The People of God also share in the prophetic role of Christ. Anointed by the Holy Spirit and guided by the sacred teaching authority of the Church and in obedience to it, they cannot err in matters of belief because they are receiving, not the mere word of men, but truly the Word of God.

It is not only through the sacraments that the Holy Spirit makes the people holy. He distributes special graces as He wills (cf. Cor. 12:7) to people of every rank. By these graces, He prepares us to undertake special tasks for the Church: "To each person the manifestation of the Spirit is given for a common good" (1 Cor. 12:7). These special gifts or charisms should be received with thanksgiving and consolation since they are useful for the "building up" of the Church. Those who shepherd the Church should judge the genuineness of these gifts, being careful not to extinguish the Spirit.

13. All men are called to belong to the new People of God which is to spread itself throughout the whole world and must exist in all ages so that God's design may be fulfilled. For all men are called to salvation by the grace of God.

Though there are many nations there is but one People of God, citizens of a heavenly rather than an earthly kingdom. All of the faithful, seeded throughout the world with different traditions, are in communion with each other in the Holy Spirit. This characteristic of being universal is a special gift of the Lord to His Church.

Not only is the Church composed of different peoples and traditions, but also of particular churches which retain their own traditions. The Pope presides over the whole assembly of charity and protects legitimate differences, taking care that these differences contribute toward unity. All men are called to be part of this Catholic unity which promotes universal peace in the Spirit of Christ.

14. We turn our attention first to the Catholic faithful. The Church, a pilgrim on earth, teaches she is necessary for salvation through Christ, the one mediator and way of salvation. He Himself clearly asserted the necessity of Baptism and of the Church, which men enter through Baptism as through a door. Whoever, knowing that the Church is made by Christ a necessary means, yet refuses to enter or remain in it, cannot be saved.

Fully incorporated in the Church are all those who accept with faith all the means of salvation which the Church offers by way of the sacraments and teaching through her ecclesiastical government of the Pope and bishops. However those who, though incorporated in the Church, fail to respond to Christ's grace and so belong just bodily to the Church, and not with faith and charity, are not saved but will be more severely judged.

Those receiving instruction in the faith or catechumens by their desire to be members are already joined to the Church, and she embraces them with love and solicitude.

15. The Church is joined in many ways to other Christians who do not profess the Catholic faith in its entirety or are not in communion with the Pope. These truly Christian people are sealed by Baptism, which unites them to Christ, and receive sacraments in their own churches. Many of them cultivate a devotion to the Virgin Mother of God and celebrate the Eucharist under the guidance of their bishops. These Christians are indeed in some real way joined to us in the Holy Spirit who stirs up a desire that all disciples of Christ may be united as Christ intended as a sign of His abiding presence among us.

16. We are related to those many peoples who have not yet received the Gospel. First are the Jews, by divine choice a most dear people to God, from which Christ was born according to the flesh. God's plan of salvation also includes Moslems, who acknowledge the Creator; they profess to hold the faith of Abraham and, together with us, they adore the one merciful God.

Those who, through no fault of their own, do not know Christ or His Church but seek God with a sincere heart by striving to do His will according to their conscience, also may attain eternal salvation. Nor does Divine Providence deny the help necessary for salvation to those who, without blame on their part, have not yet arrived at an explicit knowledge of God, but strive to lead good lives. So whatever good and truth they may have is in preparation of the Gospel.

But very often there are some left in a state of hopelessness; deceived by the Evil One, they turn their backs on God. Instead of serving God, they idolize their own sinful ways and sadly live and die without God. In her earnest desire to save all the Church takes zealous care to foster the missions—"those who are far off" that they too might "draw near" to the Lord.

17. As the Father sent the Son in mission, so Christ sends the Apostles saying, "Go, therefore, and make disciples of all the nations. Baptize them in the name of the Father, and of the Son, and of the Holy Spirit. Teach them to carry out everything I have commanded you. And know that I am with you always, until the end of the world" (Mt. 28:19-20).

The Church has received this solemn command of Christ from the Apostles and she must fulfill it to the very ends of the earth. As disciples of Christ we both laity and clergy have the obligation of spreading the faith with love and zeal to the best of our abilities.

CHAPTER III
The Organization of the Church: The College of Bishops (Episcopate)

18. To foster the continual growth of His Church, Christ established a variety of ways to serve the People of God and intended that men with sacred powers carry out these functions of service. In union with the

teaching of the First Vatican Council, we declare that Jesus Christ founded His Church through sending out Apostles just as He had been sent by the Father. He intended that the Apostles' role of service should be continued through their successors, called bishops, until the end of time. To provide a lasting and visible source for their unity, He appointed blessed Peter as their head. We, the present Council, will explain the special role of bishops who, as successors of the Apostles, together with the Pope, the Bishop of Rome, govern the house of God.

19. The Lord Jesus chose twelve of His disciples whom He sent to preach the kingdom of God just as God had sent Him. He assembled these twelve, called Apostles, in the form of a permanent group or "college" and at their head He placed Blessed Peter. Strengthening them with His own power, Christ sent them to the nations to make disciples of all peoples, to sanctify them and govern them until the end of the world.

In the power of the Holy Spirit, according to the Lord's promise, they preached the Gospel everywhere. So was gathered together the universal Church, founded upon the Apostles and built upon Peter as the chief and Christ Himself as the cornerstone.

20. In order that the preaching of the Gospel, which is the source of the Church's life, might be handed on after their deaths, the Apostles appointed successors to themselves and passed on the duty of shepherding the whole Church. They also authorized that, on their successors' deaths, other approved men should take up their ministry. Chief among

the ministries of the ancient Church was the office of bishops who, as early successors of the Apostles, passed on this ministry in unbroken succession from the Apostles to present-day bishops. With the help of priests and deacons, the bishops serve the community by teaching, sanctifying, and governing the People of God. We, gathered in Council, teach that, by the will of Christ Himself, bishops have succeeded to the place of the Apostles as shepherds of the Church. The proper title of this office of bishops is the *episcopate*.

21. The Lord Jesus Christ is present among the believers in the bishops and through their service He unites new members to His Body and continually teaches, sanctifies, and leads His pilgrim people to eternal happiness. To ensure the fulfillment of so lofty a mission, Christ empowered the Apostles with a special outpouring of His own Holy Spirit. This sacred power they have imparted to their successors by the "laying on of hands." From a universal tradition we know that through the ceremony of imposition of hands and the words of consecration, a bishop receives the grace of the Holy Spirit to carry out Christ's role of Teacher, Shepherd and High Priest. This rite, called "episcopal consecration," is the sacred ceremony for handing on the fullness of the Sacrament of Orders, a true high priesthood. Furthermore, bishops have the power to admit new members to the "college" of bishops through this sacrament.

22. Just as Christ desired that Peter and the other Apostles form a unique group or

"college," so in the same way it is the Lord's wish that Pope and bishops be united in bearing witness to the Gospel. Ecumenical councils held through the centuries show this unity of action which is called "collegiate." Indeed, every time a person becomes a bishop it is done by the imposing of hands of several other bishops, indicating that the new bishop belongs to this holy order by their collegiate action. Yet the college of bishops has no authority unless united with the Pope since, as Vicar of Christ and Pastor of the entire Church, the Pope has full, supreme, and universal power over the Universal Church. Still, the college of bishops, as successor to the college of the Apostles, together with the Pope, and never without him, has, over the whole Church, supreme and full power.

23. But this power can be exercised only with the consent of the Pope for the Lord made Simon Peter alone the rock, the keeper of the keys, and the shepherd of the flock. While expressing the rich diversity of the People of God, this college of bishops yet holds fast under one head to the unity of the one flock. Within this unity the bishops exercise their own authority for the good of the faithful. When united in an ecumenical Council, in a special way they carry out their care for the whole Church. There is never a genuine ecumenical council unless it is confirmed by the Pope for he alone has the authority to call a council into being and preside over it. Also, the Pope can call for a collegiate decision of all bishops living in different parts of the world.

According to the model of the entire Church, in which the Pope is the visible source of unity, each bishop is the foundation of unity in his particular church and represents his own church within the bonds of unity of the entire Church. Individual bishops are given charge of particular churches and govern a portion of the faithful entrusted to them. Nevertheless, each bishop, as a successor of the Apostles, is commanded by Christ to have a devoted concern for the whole Church. So, it is the duty of all bishops to spread the faith and make the light of full truth dawn on all men. The task of proclaiming the Gospel everywhere calls bishops to work together with one another and with the Pope in a community effort. They should energetically extend their help and that of their faithful to the missions, supplying workers for the harvest and material aid as well. Let them give fraternal aid to other churches in need.

We recognize with love those groupings of churches which in the course of time have grown from the ancient church centers of the East founded, as many were, by the Apostles and their successors. United together under their own disciplines and liturgical usage as well as theological and spiritual heritage, they retain the unity of faith and bonds of love with all in the Universal Church. In a similar way, there is a beautiful witness to the catholicity of the Church in those territorial unions of many churches for their mutual assistance within the Body of Christ.

24. As successors of the Apostles, bishops are sent by Christ, as they were, to teach

all nations, to preach the Gospel and to lead all to salvation by faith, Baptism and fulfillment of the commandments. Accordingly, by Christ's authority, and strengthened by the promises and graces of the Holy Spirit, they enter upon a truly apostolic ministry. As for the assignment of an individual bishop to a particular church, this can be done directly by the Pope or according to legitimate custom or by laws providing for such assignments.

25. Primarily bishops are preachers of the faith who lead all to Christ; thus among their chief duties is the preaching of the Gospel. As authentic teachers they unfold what must be believed and practiced; furthermore, guided by the Holy Spirit, they make the faith ever more clear as they draw from revelation new things as well as old. They are vigilant against errors which distrub the unity of the flock. When teaching doctrines in accord with the Bishop of Rome, they speak in Christ's name and so deserve the reverence due to witnesses of divine truth. Their teaching on faith and morals requires the religious assent of the faithful. This holds good in a special way when the Pope, teaching as Vicar of Christ, makes a pronouncement regarding Catholic truth. Here all the faithful are to attend with reverence to what he says and hold fast to the judgments he makes in full accord with his mind in the matter.

Although individual bishops are not infallible, yet they can teach Christ's doctrines infallibly. They do so when, in union with the Pope and with one another, they agree on a single point of doctrine which all must hold with firm assent. This is the more clearly evident in the setting of an ecumenical council.

Christ willed His Church to speak with infallible witness on all points of faith and morals as far as matters of revelation are concerned, for all matters of revelation must be guarded from error and faithfully explained. This is the meaning of the infallibility of the Pope's teaching office: that is when, as supreme teacher of the faithful who confirms the brethren in their faith (Lk. 22:32), he makes a final pronouncement on a doctrine of faith or morals. These definitive statements, made by the Pope from the fullness of his teaching authority and not from a consensus of the Church, are called "irreformable"—not ever to be reversed—since they have the solemn assurance of assistance of the Holy Spirit. Consequently, the infallibility of the Pope does not depend upon the consent of the Church since, in such a case, he speaks not as a private person but as the supreme teacher of the whole Church, and so as one on whom rests the full teaching authority of the Church of Jesus Christ. Because the Holy Spirit is ever active to preserve the unity of the faith, this gift of infallibility equally belongs to the whole body of bishops when, united with the Pope, it speaks with its full teaching authority. Every infallible statement is made to accord strictly with the content of revealed doctrine, whether preserved in the Scriptures or passed on through the ages by Tradition. It is through the proper succession of bishops, and especially by the watchful care of the Popes, that this body of revealed truth, or deposit of faith, under the guidance of the Holy Spirit, is exactly preserved and explained. Faithful to their teaching office, both Pope and the bishops strive by every means to inquire into all aspects of divine revelation so that they can clearly express its wealth of meaning. They do not, however, include in revealed truth any new public revelations.

26. Because the bishop is the focus of their unity, local congregations of the faithful are the new people called by God, and in them the Church of Christ is present. In the gathering of the faithful at the Eucharist under the ministry of the bishop, there is made clear a symbol of the love and unity of the Body of Christ. Rightly, then, it belongs to the office of the bishop to regulate the celebration of the Eucharist and all Christian worship for his diocese. So, too, bishops govern the ministry of the word and the sacraments for the sanctification of the faithful. Finally, they are to set an example for their people by a manner of life that influences all to strive, with God's help, for eternal life.

27. Bishops have their authority and sacred power for the salvation of their flock in truth and holiness, and they exercise it as a service in the name of Christ. Due to the fact that they govern by a power which is properly their own, it is their right and duty to make laws for their people and to regulate worship and the apostolate. Nor are bishops to be thought of as mere agents of the Pope, but they really possess the power of governing their people. Since they are sent by the Father to govern His family, bishops must

keep before their eyes the example of the Good Shepherd who came to serve and not to be served (cf. Mt. 20:28) and, indeed, to lay down his life for his sheep (cf. Jn. 10:11).

28. From ancient times, in accord with Christ's will, the ministry of the Church has been carried out by persons on different levels of participation: that is, by bishops, priests, and deacons. Associated with the bishops, and depending on them for the exercise of their ministry, are the priests who possess the true dignity of the priesthood. In virtue of priestly ordination they preach the Gospel and shepherd the faithful. At the celebration of the Mass, acting in the person of Christ, they join the faithful in offering the holy sacrifice of the Lord Jesus. Priests serve the faithful through the ministry of reconciliation and, by their life of prayer and ministry of the word, they guide the flock of Christ in spirit and truth.

As prudent cooperators of their bishop, priests form with him a unity of the priesthood in service of the People of God. In this unity they make their bishop, in a certain sense, present in the local congregations of the people; really his duties become theirs, his concerns for the flock theirs also. By reason of their sharing in the priesthood and mission of the bishop, priests should see in him a true father and obey him with reverence; and bishops ought to deal with their priests as with sons and friends. All priests are bound together by a genuine brotherhood which ought to inspire them to help one another in work, in their meetings, and in community life; and, having become at heart a pattern to the flock, let them witness to Christ the Good Shepherd.

Since men are joining more and more into a civic, economic and social unity, it is more necessary than ever that priests, united together under the leadership of the bishop and the Pope, wipe out every kind of division so that the human race may become a true family of God.

29. Deacons, who form the lower level of Church structure, are truly ordained, not for the priesthood but for the ministry of service. Among their more important duties are: to baptize, to distribute the Eucharist, to assist at marriages, to read the Scriptures, to instruct the faithful, to preside at prayer services, and to officiate at funerals and burials. It is for the national conferences of bishops to determine whether and when deacons should be ordained to exercise a permanent rank in the Church's ministry.

CHAPTER IV
The Lay People of God

30. Since lay people have such a vital role in Christ's mission to save the world, their special partnership in God's mystery of the Church deserves our thorough consideration. First of all, we define the word "laity" to mean those people of God who have professions and occupations in the work-a-day world and who live the ordinary social and family manner of living. Knowing full well that Christ did not intend that we as pastors of God's people should alone shoulder the whole work of mankind's salvation, we

declare our highest regard and esteem for the work of the laity in the sublime mission of the Church.

31. Since all the baptized form the people of God, the laity intimately, but in its own way, shares the "priestly," "prophetic," and "kingly" actions of Christ. Called by God to work for the sanctification of the world, they act as yeast in the world through their own lay occupations. By the testimony of their lives of faith, hope and charity, and by the witness of their Christian conscience, they shed the light of Christ and the message of His Gospel on all the affairs of men in this world.

32. In the Church not all proceed by the same path and if, by the will of Christ, some have a calling to the Religious life and others to a secular way of life, yet all share a true equality and a common dignity as sons of God through the one spiritual rebirth in Christ. "There does not exist among you Jew or Greek, slave or free man, male or female. All are *one* in Christ Jesus" (Gal. 3:28; cf. Col. 3:11). Hence we all possess as Christians one salvation, one hope and one undivided charity. Those differences in role or function that exist between the sacred ministers and the laity are brought into harmony by a unity of purpose: each needs the other for their mutual support in the Lord. So in our diversity we are all called upon by Christ to build up the Church in brotherly love and service to one another.

33. All in Baptism and in Confirmation are commissioned by Jesus Himself to serve the spiritual welfare of their fellowmen.

In the course of this saving work the laity make the Church present in those places and situations where only through the laymen she becomes the salt of the earth. Each of God's people should consider himself a living instrument of salvation "in the measure in which Christ bestows it" (Eph. 4:7). Consequently let the laity be eager for ever opportunity to collaborate closely with their bishops and priests and to act as partners of Christ the Lord in the fashioning of God's kingdom among men.

34. In the offering of the sacrifice of the Mass, lay persons share the "priestly" office of Jesus Christ as they offer up to God along with their Risen Lord the fruits of their apostolic endeavors: the joys and sorrows of family life, their daily toil, their prayers, the hardships of being sons of the Father amidst the evils of this age.

35. Christ the great Prophet endlessly fulfills His prophetic office not only through the bishops and clergy, but also through the laity. For this reason He makes lay people His witnesses and graces them with an understanding of the faith coupled with the special mission of kindling the hope of a kingdom not of this world. Married men and women express in family life the important prophetic role of Christ, in that their Christian family is like a "domestic Church" where each helps the other to attain holiness of life. Indeed all the laity share the work of spreading the Good News to all mankind, each in the ways best suited to his manner of life. Let the laity respond to God's call by deepening their life of

faith and conforming their whole persons to that wisdom which comes from God and leads back to Him.

36. Because of Christ's total obedience, the Father has raised Him to the glory of Lord of all creation. From His seat at the Father's right hand He now makes all created things subject to the Father. Christ has given this royal power of His victory to His disciples that they may conquer sin and through their service lead their brothers to His kingdom—a kingdom that liberates from all corruption to find "the path to peace" (Lk. 19:42). In response to the inspired promise: "All things are yours, and you are Christ's and Christ is God's" (1 Cor. 3:23), all the faithful must learn the deepest meaning and value of the whole world of creation and how to relate it to the praise of God.

The laity, by helping one another to live holier lives, fill the world with the spirit of Christ. By their competence in professions and occupations of a secular nature and guided by a strong Christian conscience, they will earnestly work to insure a fairer distribution of created goods among all men. As they bring their moral values to bear on culture and all human activity, they will open ever wider the doors of the Church through which the message of peace can enter the world. In our time it is really urgent that the faithful strive to harmonize those rights and religious duties which are theirs as the People of God and those civil rights and duties which they have as members of human society. In this way the spiritual work of the Church may more adequately match the troublesome conditions of the world today. Certainly any value system which attempts to form society with no regard for religion and which even attacks and destroys the religious freedom of its citizens is rightly to be rejected.

37. The laity have the right to receive all the spiritual gifts of the Church from their pastors and should openly confide in them, telling them their needs with brotherly love. An individual layman because of some outstanding expertise has the obligation and is encouraged to express his opinion in the area of his competence for the good of the Church. This should be done always in truth and the spirit of charity. With good grace let him accept the decision of genuine Church authority since it represents Christ, the teacher and shepherd of the Church. It is the duty of the laity to pray for those placed over them in the Church, for their pastors keep watch over them as having to render an account of their souls.

For their part pastors should encourage lay people to assume responsibility in the Church's life and should with confidence assign duties to them allowing free room for action on their own initiative. We expect many benefits from the forging of closer ties of cooperative action between the laity and their pastors.

38. In conclusion each individual lay person must be a witness to the resurrection and life of the Lord Jesus and as a sign that God lives among us. To the best of his ability let each diffuse in the world the spirit of Christ; what the soul is to the body, may Christians become to the world.

CHAPTER V
Call to Holiness

39. The mystery of the Church is revealed in the holiness which Christ, the Son of God, imparts to her in His love and desire to sanctify her. As members of this one Body of Christ, all the faithful are called to holiness, "It is God's will that you grow in holiness" (1 Thes. 4:3; cf. Eph. 1:4). Through the fruits of grace produced by the Spirit the faithful express their holiness of life as they strive for an ever more perfect love of God and neighbor. Outstanding witnesses to holiness are the lives of those who live according to the counsels of the Gospel—the "evangelical" counsels as they are called.

40. Jesus, the divine Teacher, calls everyone to holiness of life regardless of his situation. "You must be made perfect, as your Heavenly Father is perfect" (Mt. 5:48). He sent the Holy Spirit upon all men that He might inspire them from within to love God with their whole heart, with their whole soul, with all their mind, with all their strength, and to love one another as Christ loved us (cf. Jn. 13:34; 15:12). Through their Baptism, the followers of Christ are called by God, not according to their own accomplishments, but according to the designs of His heart. By His favor they truly become sons of God and are really made holy. As they live this call to holiness in the perfection of charity and seek to do the will of the Father in all things, they promote a more human and just way of life in the societies of our world.

41. There are many and varied ways of practicing this holiness: by walking unhesi-

tantly according to one's own personal gifts and by carrying out one's duties of a living faith which inspires hope and works through love. In the first place, bishops, the shepherds of Christ's flock, together with their priests, carrying out their ministry with holiness, eagerness, humility and courage, make their ministry the principal means of their sanctification. They grow in love for God and neighbor through their daily service of the Church, their pastoral care, and their daily example as a pattern to the flock.

A priest, by his task to pray and offer sacrifice for the people of God, by his apostolic works and by meditation, is led to higher sanctity. Let all priests, especially diocesan priests, remember that their loyal attachment and generous collaboration with their bishops greatly help their sanctification. Other clerics also share in the mission of grace as they prepare for the ministry under the watchful eye of their pastors.

In addition, there are laymen chosen by God and called by the bishops to devote themselves to a wholehearted service of the Kingdom of Christ. Married couples and Christian parents help one another to attain holiness by faithful love. They should instill in their children a love for Christian truth and a character formed by the Gospel. Widows and single persons also greatly add to the Church's holiness and apostolic work. Laborers, whose work is often toilsome, should, by their human efforts, try to perfect themselves and their fellow citizens and promote a better human society for all. Indeed, with their active charity in sharing one another's burdens, they should imitate Christ who roughened His hands with carpenter's tools and is always working with the Father for the salvation of all. By their daily work itself, workers can achieve greater apostolic sanctity.

Those who are oppressed by poverty, infirmity and sickness, as well as those who are persecuted for justice's sake, all are united in a special way to the suffering Christ for the salvation of the world. "The God of all grace, who called you to His everlasting glory in Christ, will Himself restore, confirm, strengthen, and establish those who have suffered a little while" (1 Pt. 5:10).

So all of Christ's faithful, whatever their circumstances, will grow in holiness day by day, through these various situations, provided they accept them all with faith from God and cooperate with the divine will. Through every activity they will show the love with which God has loved the world.

42. "God is love, and he who abides in love abides in God, and God in him" (1 Jn. 4:16). As God pours out His love into our hearts through the Holy Spirit, the first and most necessary gift is love by which we love God and our neighbor because of God. This, then, is the sign of the true disciple of Christ. Since there is no greater love than that one lay down his life for Christ and his brothers, those who suffer martyrdom are transformed into the image of their Lord and give the fullest proof of love.

An outstanding way to holiness in accordance with the special graces God gives each one is the observance of the evangelical counsels, traditionally enumerated as poverty, chastity, and obedience. By virginity and celibacy one becomes dedicated to God with an undivided heart (cf. 1 Cor. 7:32-34). Perfect chastity for the love of God is a stimulus to charity and a particular source of spiritual fruitfulness for the world.

All Christ's followers are to pursue holiness; hence let us see that we guide our affections rightly. Let us not be hindered in the search of perfect love by the use of worldly things or by a fondness for riches which goes against the spirit of evangelical poverty. Let us heed the apostle's advice: let those who make use of the world not get bogged down by it, for the structure of this world is passing away (cf. 1 Cor. 7:31 Greek text).

CHAPTER VI
The Life of Religious Families

43. By word and personal example the Lord Jesus showed how highly He revered a human life lived in poverty, in chastity, and under obedience. A life according to these evangelical counsels, as a special gift of Christ's Church, is endorsed by the authority of Apostles and Fathers of the Church. Consistent with her duty to foster Christian living, the Church has set up definite ways of living the life of the counsels in the form of the vows of poverty, chastity, and obedience.

Diverse forms of living the counsels have yielded a rich variety of religious families either of solitary or community living, providing for the growth of the Religious themselves and for the welfare of the whole Church. Religious persons find the security of an approved way of Christian perfection, the support of fellow Religious, and the conviction that by faithful observance of their chosen manner of life they are growing in charity. The Church rejoices that Religious life carries out her divine mission of salvation.

44. At their Baptism Christians are consecrated to God. When they vow to observe the counsels, they intensify this consecration. For they remove from their life all that might distract from growth in divine love and a more perfect worship of God. This special bond of the vows so unites the life of the Religious person to the service of God that it mirrors the perfect union of Christ and His Bride, the Church.

United by such a consecration to the mystery of the Church, the Religious answers God's special call to implant and strengthen the kingdom of Christ by a life dedicated to prayer or active works of charity.

It is the glory of this special vocation of living according to the counsels to be an outstanding witness to the kingdom already present in the midst of earthly cares. It foretells the victory of Christ who sets us free from the bonds of this present time. It keeps ever fresh the example of Christ's own life of dedication to His Father and shows the power of Christ's own Spirit at work in the Church.

45. Since the life of the counsels tends to the perfection of love of God and neighbor, it is for the proper Church authority to regulate the manner of life of the Religious state. In particular this authority approves the rules

of each Religious family and carefully fosters in each the genuine spirit of the outstanding person who originally founded the community.

Often the proper Church authority is the local bishop, but for good reasons the Pope himself may exercise his authority directly over a Religious family and its members. Nevertheless the Religious owe respect and obedience to the local bishop in all that concerns his pastoral authority over the local Church.

Not only does the Church give Religious life a special standing in her laws, but provides that her ministers witness the ceremony of the vows at a religious service. In her public prayers she begs God's graces upon her sons and daughters who bind themselves by Religious vows.

46. Let Religious men and women know that the Church wishes through them to present to all men the image of Jesus' own: a life of prayer, of proclaiming the Gospel, of service to works of mercy. And although their lives are notable for the giving up of so much that people rightly value, yet the living of the counsels fosters outstanding qualities of the human spirit: purity of heart and liberty of spirit. We go out of our way to pay tribute to men and women Religious serving God so loyally in monasteries, schools, hospitals, and in mission lands. They are the generous hearts, dear to God and man.

47. Know, our beloved Religious, that in your vocation you do much for the genuine holiness of the Church and for the greater glory of God, the Fountain of all holiness.

CHAPTER VII
The Heavenly Restoration of All Things: The Goal of the Pilgrim Church

48. The Church will reach its final goal of perfect completion only in the glory of heaven when by the power of God will come the time of renewal of all things (Acts 3:12). Then the whole human race, as well as the whole world, which is so closely related to man and achieves its destiny through him, will be perfectly renewed in Christ (cf. Eph. 1:10; Col. 1:20; 2 Pt. 3:10-13).

We are in the final stages of the world, for the promised restoration which awaits us has been irrevocably proclaimed and has already begun in Christ. This final destiny of all mankind is carried forward by the mission of the Holy Spirit working in and through the Church. It is in the Church that we learn through faith the meaning of our pilgrim life while working out our salvation by performing the tasks committed to us (cf. Phil. 2:12).

Since we do not know the hour or the day, on our Lord's advice, we must constantly stand guard. When we have completed our earthly life, we will appear "before the tribunal of Christ so that each one may receive his recompense, good or bad, according to his life in the body" (2 Cor. 5:10). At the end of the world "those who have done right shall rise to live; the evildoers shall rise to be damned (Jn. 5:29; cf. Mt. 25:46).

49. But at the present time some of the faithful are in exile here on earth, others have died and are being purified; others are in glory contemplating "in full light God Himself, three and one, as He really is." God's own word gives us this assurance of the victory of the Church: "He will give a new form to this lowly body of ours and remake it according to the pattern of his glorified body" (Phil. 3:21). When the Lord will come in His majesty and all the angels with Him (cf. Mt. 25:31), death will be destroyed and all things will be subject to Him (cf. 1 Cor. 15:26-27).

Whether still here on earth or undergoing purgation or in heaven, we are all in uninterrupted communion with one another because all having His Spirit form one Church and are bound together in Him (cf. Eph. 4:16).

The faithful in heaven who are more closely united with Christ establish the whole Church more firmly in holiness; interceding for us on earth and serving God they make up deficiencies of members of the pilgrim Church. Thus by their brotherly interest our weakness is greatly strengthened.

50. Because of the bonds linking together the whole Mystical Body, the Church from the very first ages has always cultivated the memory of the dead and has offered Masses and prayers for them. The Church has always believed that the Apostles and martyrs for the faith are most closely joined with us in Christ. She has always venerated them together with the Blessed Virgin and the Holy Angels. She has always devoutly

implored their intercession. God vividly speaks to us through His saints and gives us signs of His kingdom because not only are the saints an inspiration and an example, but our companionship with them joins us to Christ.

Our union with the Church in Heaven is effected especially in the liturgy where the power of the Holy Spirit acts upon us through the celebration of the Eucharist as we venerate the memory of the glorious ever Virgin Mary above all others, of blessed Joseph, the blessed Apostles, the martyrs, and all the saints.

51. We solemnly affirm with great devotion the ancient faith regarding the communion of saints and the dead being purified. Still we urge that excesses and defects in devotion be corrected because the veneration of saints is not a matter of many external acts, but rather the intensity of our active love. By such love we try to imitate their holiness and grow in their friendship; we seek their help in interceding with God for our needs. This, then, is the communion with the saints which enriches the worship of God.

All of us, children of our heavenly Father, make up one family in Christ whose glory it is to celebrate the eternal praises of the Most Blessed Trinity. When at His coming in glory Christ brings forth the dead who have died in Him to the resurrection of life, the whole Church in supreme charity will adore God and with one voice proclaim His honor and glory for ever and ever.

CHAPTER VIII
The Role of the Blessed Virgin Mary, Mother of God, in the Mystery of Christ and the Church

Preface

52. Because of His love for us, in order to effect our redemption, "God sent forth His Son born of a woman...so that we might receive our status as adopted sons" (Gal. 4:4-5). All the faithful united to Christ as Head of the Body which is the Church rightly revere with special honor the Virgin Mother of God, Blessed Mary.

53. At the message of the Angel, the Virgin Mary received the Word of God in her heart and in her body, and gave Life to the World. Hence she is endowed with the supreme dignity of being the Mother of the Son of God by which she is also the daughter of the Father and the temple of the Holy Spirit. Because of this eminent gift of grace she surpasses all creatures, but because she belongs to the human race she is one with all of us who are in need of salvation. The Catholic Church, taught by the Holy Spirit, honors her with filial affection as most beloved Mother of the Church.

54. We, the Council Fathers, intend to describe the special place of the Blessed Virgin in the mystery of the Incarnation by which God Himself became man, then our duties, as redeemed sons of God, toward the Mother of God who is Mother of Christ and

Mother of men especially of those who believe. We do not intend to give a complete doctrine on Mary nor decide theological opinions concerning Our Lady, who occupies a place in the Church which is highest after Christ and yet very close to us.

II. The Role of the Blessed Virgin in God's Plan of Salvation

55. The sacred Scriptures of both the Old and New Testament as well as ancient tradition set forth the role of the Mother of the Savior in God's overall design to bring men to salvation through the events of human history. From the earliest documents of the Old Testament, the figure of a woman, the mother of the Redeemer, is gradually thrown into sharper focus. After the age-long expectation of the promise, God's new plan of salvation was established: the Son of God took the nature of man from a woman that He might free man from sin.

56. God sought Mary's acceptance to become Mother of Christ so that, just as woman (Eve) contributed to the death of the race, so also woman, the Blessed Virgin Mary, should contribute to its new life. God adorned Mary from her conception with unique holiness—she is "full of grace" (cf. Lk. 1:28). She devoted herself to the person and work of her Son and, under Him and with Him, she serves the mystery of the Redemption of mankind. She was used by God, not just in a passive way, but as a freely cooperating person in the work of human salvation by her faith and obedience.

57.-58. The union of the Mother with the Son in the work of salvation is shown from the time of Christ's virginal conception in Mary's womb and throughout His life. And finally at the crucifixion, Mary was united to the sacrifice of her Son and heard Jesus' words, "Woman, behold your son," which made her mother to His disciples.

59. We see Mary in the midst of the Apostles on the day of Pentecost prayerfully imploring the gift of the Spirit, who had already overshadowed her in the Annunciation. Finally, upon completion of her life, preserved free from all guilt of original sin, the Immaculate Virgin was taken up body and soul into heavenly glory and exalted by the Lord as Queen of the universe.

III. The Blessed Virgin and the Church

60. There is only one mediator: Jesus Christ. The maternal duty of Mary toward men in no way obscures or diminishes this unique mediation of Christ, but rather shows His power. All the saving influence of the Blessed Virgin originates directly from the overflowing merits of Christ and in no way impedes the immediate union of the faithful to Christ but rather fosters this union.

61. God had planned for the Blessed Virgin to become the Mother of Christ from the beginning of time. In a unique way she cooperated by her obedience, faith, and love in Christ's work of restoring supernatural life to souls. For this reason she is mother to us in the order of grace.

62. On behalf of all who are brothers and sisters of her son and still pilgrims on earth, she continues her maternal saving role by her constant intercession. Therefore the Blessed Virgin is invoked by the Church under the title of Advocate and Intercessor.

The Church clearly unfolds Mary's role as subordinate to Christ's redeeming work. With her maternal help she brings us closer to the one and only Mediator and Redeemer.

63. Through her divine motherhood Mary is also intimately united with the Church. She is the perfect model of all that God wants the Church to be. She is Mother and Virgin in matters of faith, obedience, love, and perfect union with Christ. By faith and obedience she brought forth the Son of God, a Virgin made fruitful by the overshadowing of the Holy Spirit.

64. The Church, imitating Mary, becomes herself a mother. By Baptism she brings forth her children to a new and immortal life. The Church, like Mary, is a most pure virgin by the fidelity she pledged to her Spouse, the Lord Jesus.

65. Mary entered deeply into the history of salvation and in a way unites, in her person, the central truths of faith. When she is the subject of devotion, she summons the faithful to her Son. She is the model for all followers of Christ to increase in holiness by conquering sins. In her own life, she lived an example of that maternal love which should animate all of us as collaborators in the mission of the Church.

IV. Devotion to the Blessed Virgin in the Church

66. Mary has been exalted above all angels and men to a place second only to her Son as the most holy Mother of God, who was involved in the mysteries of Christ. Since the earliest times the devotion by the People of God toward Mary has always grown in love, veneration, and imitation, according to her own prophetic words, "All ages to come shall call me blessed. God who is mighty has done great things for me" (Lk. 1:48). This reverence for Mary differs essentially from the adoration offered to Christ, the Father, and the Holy Spirit. The various forms of loving devotions toward the Mother of God which the Church encourages, especially in the liturgy, should be generously fostered and treasured within the bounds of sound doctrine. While honoring Christ's mother, these devotions cause her Son to be rightly known, loved, and imitated.

67. We exhort all the faithful to foster liturgical practices honoring the Mother of God and to observe with great care the decrees concerning the images of Christ, the Blessed Virgin and the saints. We earnestly exhort theologians and preachers of the Word of God that, in treating of the unique dignity of the Mother of God, they carefully refrain from false exaggeration on the one hand and the excess of narrow-mindedness on the other.

As models of sound teaching, the holy Fathers and the doctors of the Church, under the teaching authority of the Church, explain the role and the privileges of the Blessed Virgin, which are always related to Christ. Let those who teach and preach guard against any word or deed which could lead separated brethren, or anyone else, into error regarding the true doctrine of the Church, for true devotion proceeds from true faith.

V. Mary a Sign of Sure Hope and of Solace for God's People in Pilgrimage

68.-69. It gives us great joy and comfort that among the separated brethren, too, there are those who give due honor to the Mother of our Lord and Savior. This is so especially among Christians living in the Near East who, with ardent emotion and devout mind, honor the Mother of God. Let the entire body of the faithful persevere in prayer to the Mother of God and Mother of men. Let us pray that she who aided the beginnings of the Church on earth by her prayers may now, exalted as she is in heaven above all the saints and angels, intercede with her Son together with all the saints. May all families of peoples of the world be happily gathered together in peace and harmony into one People of God for the glory of the most Holy and Undivided Trinity.

Constitution on the Liturgy

(Sacrosanctum Concilium, December 4, 1963)

A paraphrase by
Rev. C. J. McNaspy, S.J.

1. We, the Fathers of the Second Vatican Council, have decided to treat first of all the matter of Christian worship or liturgy; and this for several reasons. In the first place, in the liturgy the work of our redemption is accomplished. Thus we have received the outstanding means of expressing in our lives the mystery of Christ and what the Church really is.

2. For the Church is both human and divine. It is something seen on earth, yet full of unseen gifts. It is eager to act, yet given to prayer and contemplation. It is in the world, yet not fully at home in it.

The liturgy strengthens our Christian lives, and at the same time it is a sign to the whole world — a sign of what Christianity really is (Is. 11:12; Jn. 11:52; Jn. 10:16).

3.-4. In this Council we aim at intensifying our Christian living; but we also aim at adaptation of the tradition, making the liturgy more responsive to today's needs. Some of our Christian worship comes from God and cannot be changed by human beings. But what is human — the development of the Church — can and should be adapted to meet the human needs of our times.

CHAPTER I

5. We are saved through Christ, the Mediator between God and human beings. Christ did this work mainly by dying, rising and ascending into heaven. This is the paschal mystery.

6.-7. As the Father sent Christ, Christ sent the Apostles. They were to preach the Gospel and continue the work of salvation through sacrifice and sacraments. Christ is always present in His Church, especially in the great moments of the liturgy — in the Sacrifice of the Mass (especially in the Eucharistic species), in His word, and "where two or three are gathered" for His sake in prayer and singing (Mt. 18:20).

8. In the liturgy, too, we have a foretaste, an anticipation, of the worship of God in heaven. Here on earth we are pilgrims toward the heavenly city (Rev. 21:2; Col. 3:1; Heb. 8:2).

9. Not that liturgy is everything, of course. Before we can worship God fully, we are called to faith and to conversion. Even Christians are not perfect; they need to be called again and again to faith and conversion.

10. At the same time, the liturgy is called "the summit" toward which our activity as Christians is aimed. It is also "the fountain" of Christian life and grace. In it God is glorified and mankind made holy.

11. This means, of course, that we Christians are called not merely to be present, but to take part in the liturgy and understand what we are doing.

12.-13. But even this is not everything. Christ tells us also to pray in private, "in secret," in fact, to "pray always." This means that other forms of prayer and devotion are good, too. But the liturgy should be the center of all.

II. Taking Part in Worship

14. The Church urges us to take part in worship, as fully and actively and with as much understanding as possible. This is our

right and our duty as baptized Christians — called by St. Peter "a chosen race, a royal priesthood, a holy nation, a people He claims for His own" (1 Pt. 2:9; 2:4-5).

15.-18. This means, obviously, that priests must understand fully what they are doing as leaders of the liturgy. They must be well educated in liturgy if they are to help others. For this reason, it is vital that seminary education be so structured that a thorough training in the spirit of the liturgy be imparted: its theological, historical, spiritual, pastoral, and ritual aspects. Professors of other theological sciences are to make clear the close association of their areas of learning with the liturgy. Throughout the seminary training young men are to be led through experiencing the liturgical rites as well as studying them to a deep love of liturgical worship.

19.-20. So it is that pastors are urged to share this knowledge with their people and to promote real participation. They should be considerate of the people's needs, considering their age, education, and background. Let prudent use be made of the broadcasting and televising of liturgical actions, especially of the Mass.

III. Reforming the Liturgy

21. As said above, liturgy is partly given by God and partly developed by human beings. God's part cannot be changed by us, but the human part can be, and sometimes should be.

22. For this reason, by our authority as a Church Council we are making some

changes. But anything as important as the liturgy is obviously too precious to be handled by just anybody. This is the responsibility of the Pope and the bishops.

23. Even so, it is a good idea for all Christians to understand what norms will be used in making changes.

24.-25. Holy Scripture is a central part of worship, and the main changes in our worship have to do with Holy Scripture. The revised Lectionary (or book of scriptural readings) now in use offers a wide range of sacred history and gives us, over the years, a fuller grasp of God's dealings with mankind.

26.-32. Another principle for changing the liturgy is the central fact that the liturgy is not a private affair, but the public celebration of the entire Church. This implies different roles: that of priest, for example, that of reader, of singer, and the like. While everybody is called on to participate, not everybody does everything. The reason for this is the community nature of the Church which requires of course a worshiping group. But even more, each one—minister, server, reader, singer—does only his own part; he should do it well and with real devotion. The body of the community, too, are to be active: by song, gesture, bodily posture, even silence. These actions of the lay people in the rites of the Church are now clearly set down as their active part in the worship of God.

33. The liturgy has an educational function, too. Like the Council itself, it has a "pastoral" bent, for the good of the people.

34. Thus, especially in this period of time, ceremonies should be somewhat simple,

though dignified; they should be short, clear, and without too much repetition. They should be clear enough not to require much explanation.

35. The sermon should be a "homily" — that is, not simply a talk about some religious subject, but closely related to the scriptural readings of the day. The sermon is not a separate ceremony, but part of the liturgy.

36. We officially open the way to the language of the people, the vernacular, for use in the sacred rites of the Church. This applies with good sense to readings, prayers and chants. We leave to the authority of National Conferences of Bishops to decide to what extent the vernacular is to be used in the liturgy and to have it approved by the Pope's authority.

37.-40. Since the Church is made up of people of diverse lands, language, and culture, it is fitting that she address her worship to God in the overtones of this rich diversity. She is happy to bring into liturgical celebrations whatever cultural elements may genuinely adorn the fitting worship of God and encourages such adaptations in her rites as are necessary for making all her children at home in their Father's house. These adaptations of language and rites she entrusts to the national conferences of bishops to work out with their experts and submit to the Pope for approval.

IV. Liturgical Life in Diocese and Parish

41. Whatever else he may have to do, the bishop is there principally as high priest of the people. This can be seen most effective-

ly in ceremonies where the bishop is celebrating in company with his priests.

42. But in everyday spiritual life, the focus will be on the parish, where the pastor or pastors take the place of the bishop. The common celebration of Sunday Mass is the center of parish life.

V. Promoting Pastoral-Liturgical Action

43.-46. We have no doubt that a determination to breathe new life into the Church's liturgy is a movement of the Spirit in our time. So we urge the following:

Committees for the promotion of worship should be set up by bishops, bringing in experts in the field. Experimental programs should be studied and proposed to the right authorities. Dioceses, too, should have committees of experts on sacred music and sacred art.

CHAPTER II

47. At the Last Supper, our Savior instituted the Eucharistic Sacrifice to continue His sacrifice until He comes again. The Eucharist is thus a sacrifice, a sacrament of love, a sign of unity, a bond of charity, a pledge of future glory.

48. At Mass, then, the faithful should not be here "as strangers or silent spectators." They should understand what is going on and participate intelligently and actively.

49.-50. Accordingly, the ceremonies of the Mass are to be simplified and made more understandable. Repetitiousness should be avoided, and we should return to something of the simplicity of the early Church.

51. A richer selection of Holy Scripture should be offered, and by means of the homily the faith and principles of Christian life should be explained "from the sacred text during the course of the liturgical year."

52.-53. Following the homily, the "common prayer" or "prayer of the faithful" should be restored. This is another opportunity for the people to take part.

54. While the vernacular or "mother tongue" is now allowed in the liturgy, we encourage people also to learn to say or sing in Latin those parts that are properly belonging to the people.

55.-56. Frequent communion is encouraged, especially from the very "elements consecrated at that very sacrifice." Communion under "both species"—the host and the cup—is allowed, at least when the bishops judge it good for the people.

57. Concelebration—or the celebration of several priests at the same time—is proposed by the Council at least for certain appropriate occasions.

58. The union of the two parts—the liturgy of the word and liturgy of Eucharist—forms the unity of one action of worship.

CHAPTER III

The Other Sacraments and Sacramentals

59. Christ instituted the sacraments to make people holy, to build up the Body of Christ, to give worship to God. They also instruct, and should be easily understood.

60. The Church has instituted other ceremonies that look a bit like sacraments

and are meant to be helpful to the people. These are called "sacramentals."

61.-62. The sacraments especially, and the sacramentals to a lesser degree, help us to make important events of our lives more holy. For this it is necessary to revise these ceremonies and make them more relevant to us.

63. We now allow the use of the mother tongue in the sacraments and sacramentals, and call for new ceremonies that will prove more effective.

64.-70. First there is the sacrament of "initiation" of Baptism. New, richer ceremonies are to be provided, together with a considerable time of preparation for adults about to be baptized. Special ceremonies are to be celebrated—with suitable differences—in the baptisms of adults, of infants, of a group, of converts and of those baptized in emergencies.

71. The second sacrament of initiation, called "Confirmation," is to be made more expressive in a revised ceremony.

72. The sacrament of "reconciliation"—or Penance—is also to be revised in order to make it more expressive of its deep meaning.

73.-75. The "Sacrament of the Sick"—which is also called Extreme Unction—should be given not at the point of death but as soon as the Christian begins to be in danger of death from sickness or old age. This is to include provision for confession and the reception of Viaticum.

76.-78. Ceremonies pertaining to the sacrament of Holy Orders, too, should be made more intelligible and effective, and the same is said of the sacrament of Matrimony. Matrimony should be normally celebrated at Mass during which a homily is proper and the prayer for the bride is recited.

79.-82. The sacramentals, too, are to be revised in order to make them more meaningful. This includes the ceremony of Christian burial, which should stress the meaning of the resurrection and the whole paschal mystery.

80. The ceremonies surrounding the vows in Religious life should be made more simple and dignified, and they, too, should normally be done during Mass.

CHAPTER IV

The Divine Office

83.-86. Jesus, our high priest, continues His prayer to the Father through His Church as she offers her prayers of praise and petition in an organized way called the Divine Office. From the early days of the Church, Christians have sung these divine praises at all hours of the day and even during the night, following Christ's command to "pray always." Priests especially, together with monks, nuns and others, are especially commissioned to carry on this important Christian task. They stand in prayer before God in the name of Mother Church.

87. In today's world, however, it is impossible for priests involved in the active ministry to follow a schedule of strictly contemplative monks, among whom the "prayer of the hours" began.

88. In the reform of the "Divine Office," as this official prayer is called, we call for

an arrangement of psalms and other prayers and readings to fit the real needs and real possibilities of those whose duty it is to pray "the hours."

89.-94. Prayers suitable for morning and evening praise of God will be the basis for the Office. Then an arrangement of readings from Scripture, from ancient spiritual writers, from modern works, and from the lives of the saints—all will find a place in this official prayer of the Church. Finally shorter selections, chiefly from the psalms, will be provided for brief periods of prayer during the course of the day.

Since the purpose of the Office is to provide solid spiritual nourishment for the prayer life of priests and others who recite it, those who pray the psalms and readings from the Bible must come to appreciate their meaning by preparatory study.

95.-99. The ideal way to celebrate the Divine Office is by singing and reciting in choir. This is the way monks, nuns, and other Religious families pray the divine Hours. Those members of Religious orders and priests who recite the Office privately are also offering the official prayer of the Church; they, too, are encouraged to a group recitation of at least part of the Office.

100.-101. Lay men and women, too, are encouraged to participate in this official prayer of the Church. As in the Mass, scriptural readings are to be made representative of the entire word of God, and the Divine Office is to be made more spiritually useful to all, especially by the use of good translations in vernacular languages.

CHAPTER V
The Liturgical Year

102. Every Sunday, the Lord's day, is specially dedicated to reliving the resurrection.

During the course of the year, however, the liturgy unfolds the whole mystery of Christ—His incarnation, birth, death, resurrection, ascension, as well as the coming of the Holy Spirit at Pentecost.

In these celebrations, the great mysteries are "in some way made present," and the faithful are able to grasp them better and be filled with the appropriate grace of each mystery.

103. In the annual cycle of Christ's mysteries, the Church honors with special love the Mother of God, who is closely bound into the saving work of Christ. In her we joyfully recall Mary as a faultless model of what we desire to be.

104. During the year, too, we remember the martyrs and other saints who have been redeemed by Christ and who are examples to the rest of us.

105. Finally, the year offers special times of penance and prayer for mercy.

106. Once again we call for reform in the direction of clarity and simplicity. Stress is placed on Sunday as the celebration of Christ's resurrection.

107.-108. The liturgical year, in line with this reform, is being restored "to meet the conditions of modern times." The focus of the faithful's attention is primarily on the feasts of the mysteries of salvation.

109.-110. Lent, the time of special penance, is one of special instruction, too. We are to realize better both the social consequences of sin and the fact that sin is an offence against God.

111. So that celebration of the saints' feast days might not obscure the central mysteries of our faith, we urge cutting down on the number of such celebrations. Instead, we are to stress only those saints that have a special significance to our local communities and those that are "of universal significance."

CHAPTER VI

Sacred Music

112. Sacred music is a special art, since in it melody is united to sacred words. It thus has a "ministerial function."

Sacred music performs its function better when it is closely linked with liturgical action, expressing prayerfulness, uniting us in community, and adding solemnity to ceremonies.

113. Liturgical action is "given a more noble form" when made more solemn in song and the participation of the people.

114. The Church has a great "treasure of sacred music," and this must not be neglected but fostered. Choirs are not to be dropped, but to be "diligently promoted." But the whole congregation, too, must be involved. Let Catholic education at every level include training in sacred song.

115.-118. Several kinds of sacred music must be mentioned. The ancient Gregorian chant "should be given pride of place." But other kinds of sacred music, especially great choral (polyphonic) music are welcomed, too.

119. In various parts of the world, especially mission lands, there exist special musical traditions that are very important to the people. To this, too, "a suitable place is to be given."

120. The pipe organ is especially held "in high esteem," since it is both traditional and able to "add a wonderful splendor" to worship. But other instruments are admitted also, when they are used in accord with the dignity of the Church and help the faithful to pray.

121. Composers are encouraged to "cultivate sacred music and increase its store of treasures." They are urged especially to write music that congregations and smaller choirs can sing, and to draw their texts "chiefly from Holy Scripture and from liturgical sources."

CHAPTER VII

Sacred Art and Architecture

122. As a Council we praise the fine arts as "among the noblest expressions of human genius." This is especially the case with sacred art, expressing God's beauty.

The Church "has always been the friend of the fine arts and sought their noble ministry." It has always been careful to make sure that architecture and church furnishings should serve the dignity of worship.

123. No particular style of art is exclusively used by the Church. The art of our own

day "shall be given free scope," provided that it does its task with due honor and reverence.

124. Sacred art should "strive after noble beauty rather than mere extravagance."

When churches are to be built, they should be well adapted to liturgical needs, especially to active participation by the faithful.

125. Sacred images are fine, as long as their number is moderate and as long as their placing "reflects right order." Otherwise they can be distracting or confusing and promote a faulty sense of devotion.

126.-130. In building or adorning churches, the Church should take advice from experts. In turn, bishops should help artists to understand the spirit of sacred art and the liturgy. All priests should learn something about the history and development of sacred art. This way, they will be able to appreciate and preserve good sacred art of the past and be "in a position to aid, by good advice, artists who are engaged in producing" new works of art.

Decree on Eastern Catholic Churches

(Orientalium Ecclesiarum,
November 21, 1964)

A paraphrase by
Rev. Robert Ference

Introduction

1. The Eastern Catholic Churches are held in high esteem for the riches of their ancient traditions which were handed down from the Apostles and which form part of the revealed heritage of the one undivided Church. In our concern that the Eastern Churches may be preserved, continue to grow, and carry out the mission entrusted to them, we set down a number of principles in their regard.

Individual Churches or Rites

2. The Catholic Church is made up of faithful who are united by the same faith, the same sacraments, the same hierarchy, but form separate rites, that is, ways of worshiping the one Lord within their own traditions. One admirable brotherhood flourishes among them giving witness to the universality of the Church. It is our desire that each individual Church or rite retain its own traditions completely while adapting to modern times.

3. All these Churches, whether from the East or the West, are equally entrusted to the pastoral guidance of the Pope but enjoy an equality of dignity, rights, and duties among themselves. So that the traditions of these Churches might be preserved, parishes and a special hierarchy should be established for each according to need. The leading bishops of the individual Church rites in the same territory should promote unity of action. Clerics and laity alike should be well instructed in various rites and their rules.

4. Each Eastern rite Catholic as well as any baptized non-Catholic who fully embraces

the Catholic Church should retain the worship of his own rite.

The Spiritual Heritage of the Eastern Churches

5. The universal Church clearly manifests how indebted she is to the Eastern Churches for their spiritual heritage and looks upon this as the heritage of Christ's universal Church. Consequently we declare that the churches of the East as well as those of the West enjoy the right and duty to rule themselves.

6. We exhort all Easterners (so we refer to members of the Eastern Churches) to preserve and honor their liturgical rites and way of life with great fidelity. Let those Easterners who have abandoned their traditions take great pains to return to their ancestral ways. Religious societies of the Latin rite working among Eastern faithful are strongly counseled to found houses or provinces of Eastern rites wherever possible.

Patriarchs of the Eastern Churches

7.-8. From the earliest times the institution of the patriarchate existed. The Eastern patriarch is the bishop who has jurisdiction over all other bishops, clergy, and people of his own territory or rite, without prejudice to the authority of the Pope. All patriarchates, even those of later origin, are of equal dignity, yet the honorary ranking among them is to be retained.

9.-11. Each patriarch presides over his patriarchate as father and head and as such he is to be honored and respected. Therefore we decree that his rights and privileges, dating from before the division of East and West, should be re-established according to ancient traditions. The patriarch with his synod or council constitutes the superior authority in each patriarchate, with power to nominate bishops of the particular rite within his territorial boundaries. These same principles apply also to major archbishops. It is our desire that where needed new patriarchates be established either by the authority of a council or a Pope.

Rules for the Sacraments

12.-14. We fully endorse the ancient practices of conferring the sacraments and earnestly wish them to be restored. The priest, for instance, may administer the sacrament of Holy Chrism (Confirmation) with oil blessed by the patriarch or bishop. All Eastern rite priests can confer this sacrament along with Baptism or even separately to all the faithful of any rite including the Latin. And priests of the Latin rite may with prescribed faculties, confer this sacrament to Eastern rite faithful.

15. On Sundays and feast days the faithful are bound to attend the divine liturgy or Divine Praises. It is permitted that this obligation may be fulfilled from the Vespers of the Vigil to the end of Sunday or feast day.

16. The bishop of a territory can grant a priest of any rite the faculty of hearing confession from the faithful of any rite unless the local bishop of another rite determines otherwise for his priests.

17. We also desire that the ancient office of the deacon be restored. It is for each individual church to determine the usefulness of the subdiaconate and the minor orders.

18. For the sake of the sanctity of marriage between Eastern Catholics and baptized Eastern non-Catholics, we decree that the presence of a sacred minister at such marriages is sufficient for their validity.

Divine Worship

19. Either an ecumenical council or Papal authority has the exclusive right to suppress, transfer, and establish feast days for all the Eastern Churches. However for feasts of individual churches it is within the competence of a patriarchal or archiepiscopal council to legislate.

20.-21. It is for the patriarchs to decide on a single Sunday of the year for the observance of Easter. As for sacred seasons the faithful are permitted to observe those of any rite in the place where they live.

22. We encourage the celebration of Divine Praises, not only by clerics and Religious, but by the lay faithful as well.

23. The patriarchs have the right to regulate the use of languages, even vernacular languages, in liturgical functions after making a report on the matter to Roman authorities.

Relations with the Separated Churches

24. The Eastern Churches in communion with Rome are entrusted with the special mission of promoting the unity of all Chris-

tians particularly the Easterners. Let them carry out this work by prayer and by religious fidelity to ancient traditions which manifest to our separated brethren that Church unity can be affected without the particular churches losing their individual characteristics.

25. If any separated Eastern Christian should join himself to Catholic unity, all he is required to give is a simple profession of Catholic faith. Clerics of other churches of the East are permitted to exercise the orders they possess.

26. With respect to separated Eastern brethren we formulate a milder policy regarding common worship especially where the eternal good of souls is at stake. To promote a closer union with these churches we set the following norms:

27. If any of our Eastern brethren of separated churches ask, they may be granted the sacraments of Penance, Eucharist, and Anointing of the Sick. Also Catholics may ask for these same sacraments from the Eastern Christian ministers whenever necessity or a genuine spiritual benefit recommends and when access to a Catholic priest is physically or morally impossible.

28. Further, Catholics may join with their separated Eastern brethren in sacred functions and prayer services.

29. This policy in regard to common worship among Catholics and baptized Eastern non-Catholics is entrusted to cooperative arrangements between the local bishops and the bishops of the separated Eastern Churches.

30. All these directions of law are laid down for the present situation until such time as the Catholic Church and the separated Eastern Churches come together into complete unity. In the meanwhile all Christians, Eastern and Western, are asked to pray fervently and insistently to God, that with the aid of the most holy Mother of God all may become one in Christ.

Decree on Ecumenism

(Unitatis Redintegratio,
November 21, 1964)

A paraphrase by
Rev. Harold B. Bumpus

Introduction

1. Promoting unity among all Christians is one of our chief concerns in the Second Vatican Council. Discord contradicts the will of Christ for us and hinders the preaching of the Good News. Everywhere large numbers of Christians, Catholics and separated brethren alike, have felt the grace of the Holy Spirit leading to the restoration of unity. In this Council we wish to set a tone, offer certain helps, and provide pathways and methods for Catholics by which they can respond to the Divine Call.

CHAPTER I

Catholic Principles on Ecumenism

2. The love of God is revealed to us because He sent His only Son into the world in order that all might possess new life and unity (cf. 1 Jn. 4:9; Col. 1:18-20; Jn. 11:52; Jn. 17:21). *The Eucharist both signifies that unity and that new life and brings them about.* All were called in one hope of our calling (Eph. 4:4-5), and the Holy Spirit is sent to bring it about. It is He who enriches the Church of Jesus Christ with its different functions.

In order to establish the Church throughout the world until the end of time, Christ entrusted to His twelve followers the task of teaching, ruling, and sanctifying, with Peter possessing the keys of the kingdom and a sacred trust for all His sheep, Jesus Himself remaining the chief cornerstone and shepherd of souls.

It is through faithful preaching of the Word, dedicated administration of the sacraments, and loving authority that Jesus Christ wishes His people to grow on their spiritual journey to God. The Church ministers in this threefold fashion as it makes its pilgrim way to the kingdom of God. This is the sacred mystery of the unity of the Church: a unity that exists in Christ and is channeled through Him with the Holy Spirit energizing a variety of functions.

3. From the very beginning strife and disunion rose up in the Church, separating large communities from each other. This disunion is the result of sin into which all parties have entered at one time or another. However, the sin of separation from that unity so dear to Christ cannot be laid on the shoulders of those who in the present time are born into these separated communities. The Catholic Church accepts with respect and affection those who are believers in Jesus Christ in the separated communities, for they possess a certain, if imperfect, communion with the Catholic Church through Baptism and faith. But differences of faith statement and practice do create obstacles to full unity. Nonetheless, all those justified by faith through Baptism are united to Christ. Moreover, many of the most significant elements that give life to the Church can exist outside its visible boundaries; namely, the written Word of God, the grace of God; the virtues of faith, hope and love; the interior gifts of the Holy Spirit. The Spirit of God has used these believing communities as a means of salvation. They derive their power from the fullness entrusted

to the Catholic Church. For it alone is the all-embracing means of salvation. We believe that our Lord entrusted all the blessings of the New Covenant to the Apostles with Peter as head in order to establish one believing community on earth in union with Christ; which despite sin in the world, is growing in Christ and is being guided to fullness of life in eternal glory.

4. The Holy Spirit has already led many people through prayer, word, and action to strive for that unity which Christ desires. We therefore call upon all Catholics to recognize the signs of the times and to take an active and intelligent part in the cause of Church unity. The "ecumenical movement" means those activities and enterprises which, according to the needs of the Church and on appropriate occasions, are started for the fostering of unity among Christians. These activities include: a) eliminate words, judgments, and actions that do not represent truthfully and fairly the situation of the various believing communities; b) begin dialogue between competent experts from the different Churches, bringing out in depth the distinctive features of each group; c) cooperate more closely in whatever projects a Christian conscience dictates for the common good; and last of all come together for common prayers examining the need all have for renewal and reform.

The result of such prudent Christian sharing under the guidance of spiritual shepherds will be the spiritual blessings of justice and truth, concord and cooperation, and a spirit of brotherly love and unity. Thus all believers will finally be gathered with a spirit of concord into the common celebration of the Eucharist, manifesting that unity which Christ wishes His Church to have.

In such sharing, Catholics need to be intellectually informed and spiritually molded in the traditions of their own Church so as to make visible to others what they have received. For although the Church is endowed with all divinely revealed truth and all the means of grace, her members do not always manifest this fullness nor let the light of Christ shine before men. Every Catholic must aim at spiritual perfection (Jas. 1:4; Rom. 12:1-2), each according to his own position in life, so that the Lord may present His Church to the Father without spot or wrinkle (Eph. 5:27). On this journey unity is necessary in essentials while proper freedom in the various forms of spiritual life of worship, and theological expression is to be preserved.

Catholics should recognize and value the true Christian endowments of our separated brethren, by whom enormous love and zeal have been expended in bearing witness to Christ. What is effected by their cooperation with the grace of the Holy Spirit serves as an example to encourage and build us up in the Lord.

Nonetheless, the divisions among believers prevent the universality of the Church from being visible in those who are joined to her by Baptism, but still separated from full communion. This work of healing divisions among Christians we commend to bishops everywhere in the world.

CHAPTER II
The Practice of Ecumenism

5. Restoration of unity among Christians is the concern of all believers according to their individual talents. Every renewal in the Church is an invitation to increased devotion to her calling.

6. Christ calls the Church to that continual reformation which she always needs, because she is an institution made up of fallible human beings. And so we must respond by making good those deficiencies, be they in conduct, practice, or even in doctrinal expressions, which have sprung up over past centuries. As renewal goes forward in the biblical and liturgical movements, in education, and in social endeavors, new understandings and expressions in unity with non-Catholics take on noteworthy importance.

7. Ecumenism involves a renewal of heart, of outgoing love, and a desire for unity which is the gift of the Holy Spirit to those who call upon Him. Thus all need the grace of repentance and the grace to forgive. The more believers live by the Gospel, the more they are fostering Christian unity by example and by entering into a profound relationship with God — the source of all unity. This is rightly called spiritual ecumenism.

8. Thus Catholics should join in prayer services for unity. These services are an effective way of asking for the grace of unity as well as a way to discover the ties that bind us together. Such common prayer is not to be used indiscriminately, but should always

provide a means of sharing in grace and signifying the unity of the Church. Guidelines for ecumenical prayer are established by the local bishop.

9. To understand the outlook of our separated brethren, considerable serious study is required. Catholics need to acquire a more adequate understanding of the distinctive teachings of our separated brethren as well as firmly grasp their own religious and theological backgrounds. Meetings under competent guidance are encouraged for the purpose of friendly theological dialogue.

10. Studies in theology and history should be presented from an ecumenical perspective. Future priests and bishops should be trained in this way and not in a context of polemics, so that they may rightly instruct the faithful. In mission areas care should be taken to understand the problems and benefits that affect this work because of the ecumenical movement.

11. Catholic teaching should be presented in its entirety, so as to avoid a false conciliatory approach; but at the same time it should be couched in language all can readily understand.

In Catholic teaching there exists an order of truths by which in varying degrees they relate to the fundamentals of the faith. This order as well as the terminology used to express the truths of faith should be concerns of Catholic theologians when they engage in ecumenical dialogues.

12. Professing a common faith in the triune God and in Jesus Christ, His Son and our Savior, we bear witness to our shared

hope in Christ who came to serve and not to be served. As we serve the cause of the common family of mankind by upholding the social dignity of all mankind, we shall be drawn together by our cooperative efforts and united in our esteem for one another. This way of united service must surely lead to the goal of Christian unity.

CHAPTER III

Churches and Ecclesial Communities Separated from the Roman Catholic Church

13. In the course of history two major divisions from the See of Rome took place; namely, the division from the Eastern Churches over some dogmatic statements of early Councils or the breakdown of communications between certain Eastern Patriarchs and Rome, and secondly the divisions in the West in the period of the Reformation where great diversity of structure and of theological expression was manifested.

The Special Position of the Eastern Churches

14. Although East and West have gone their own ways in certain areas, the Patriarchal Churches of the East glory in tracing their origins to the Apostles and hence share this Apostolic heritage with each other and with Rome. From the East have come many

contributions to liturgy, theology, and law in the West. Indeed the seven early Ecumenical Councils were held in the East.

Special causes and human failing set the stage for separation, and we today must give special attention to the appropriate uniqueness of the Eastern Churches when we work to restore full communion between East and West.

15. Everyone knows with what love the Eastern Churches celebrate the Eucharist. In liturgical worship the Blessed Virgin Mary is highly commemorated, and homage is given to the saints and Fathers of the Church. These Churches possess true sacraments by Apostolic Succession; hence some common worship is not only allowed, but also recommended.

In the East one also finds the rich monastic tradition which later became popular in Europe. We strongly urge all to understand, foster, and preserve the rich inheritance we have received from the East and to work for reconciliation.

16. The Eastern Churches have always maintained their own customs and observances, all of which have aided them in carrying out their mission to the world. These Churches have the power to govern themselves according to their own needs and in their own contexts.

17. Legitimate variety exists in the formulation of faith statements or doctrine where East and West have examined different facets of the Divine Mysteries and illuminated them according to their particular genius. Such authentic traditions, rooted in Scripture and

given full expression in the liturgy of the community and in daily life, direct believers to a fuller contemplation of Christian truth. Their entire heritage belongs to the fullness of the Catholic and apostolic life.

18. We proclaim once again that no requirements beyond essentials be demanded for visible unity, and we urgently desire that every effort be made toward unity with the Churches of the East. Through prayer, fraternal dialogue on points of doctrine, and cooperation on problems of a pastoral nature we can build bridges of unity. We recommend that close ties of friendship be formed with those no longer living in the East but as foreigners in various parts of the world. Through such efforts we are confident that we can breach the wall of division between the Eastern and Western Church.

The Separated Churches and Ecclesial Communities in the West

19. Those Christians separated from Rome during the Reformation and later, are bound to the Catholic Church by the bond of long years of union and common teaching.

Since the different churches show such diversity today, we do not propose to deal with specific churches in this document, but rather we hope and pray that the ecumenical spirit and mutual esteem will grow among all men. To this end we propose some ideas to serve as a basis and motivation for further dialogue.

20. First, we rejoice to see our brethren looking to Christ whom they confess as God

and Lord and sole Mediator between God and man as source and center of ecclesiastical community. All affirm this in the face of our undoubted differences in doctrine regarding Christ's redemptive work, the ministry of the Church, and the role of Mary in the work of salvation.

21. Love and veneration of the Holy Bible among our separated brethren has led them to constant and expert study of the Scriptures where they seek God as He speaks in Jesus Christ. In Scripture they contemplate the life and work of Christ for our salvation, especially His Death and Resurrection.

But many of our brethren think differently than we do about the relationship between Church and Scripture. For Catholics, the Church is the authentic interpreter of the written word of God. But granted the variety of ways of approaching the Holy Bible as Word of God, it is still a powerful instrument in leading men to that union which Christ desires.

22. By Baptism properly conferred and properly received, a human person is joined to the glorified Christ and has a share in His divine life (Rom. 6:4; Col. 2:12). Those who are baptized, then, are joined by a common bond, while Baptism itself is the point of departure to fullness of life and faith in the Eucharist. But the separated communities lack that fullness, especially Holy Orders, and thus have not preserved the genuine and total reality of the Eucharistic mystery. Yet they do await His coming in glory when they celebrate the Lord's Supper. Therefore, we should undertake dialogue with them concern-

ing the true meaning of the Eucharist and the other sacraments so as to promote mutual understanding.

23. The Christian way of life is nourished for our separated brethren by the grace of Baptism and by hearing God's Word. By private prayer and meditation and by hearing the Word of God in public worship they further their life of faith and give praise to God. Their active faith has led them to many works of Christian charity for the good of individuals and for peace throughout the world. Although many Christians do not understand the Gospel message in the same sense that Catholics do and do not accept the same solutions to the problems of our society as Catholics do, yet they cling to Christ's words as the source of Christian life and activity (Col. 3:17). Hence ecumenical discussion could well begin with dialogue about what light the Gospel casts on moral issues of our day.

24. In seeking that unity which Christ desires, we urge that all men avoid surface judgments or imprudent behavior, concentrating rather on presenting honestly and fully the Catholic tradition to those with whom they are in dialogue. We should go forward without prejudicing the future inspiration of the Holy Spirit in the work of reconciling Christians with one another. We place full hope in the prayer of Christ for the Church, and "this hope will not leave us disappointed, because the love of God has been poured out in our hearts through the Holy Spirit who has been given to us" (Rom. 5:5).

Declaration on the Relationship of the Church to Non-Christian Religions

(Nostra Aetate, October 28, 1965)

A paraphrase by
Rev. Austin N. Park, S.J.

1. Since the Church is obliged by Christ's law of love to try to strengthen the ties that unite the different members of the human family she stressed those things that we all have in common that help us to truly become brothers. All men live in God's loving providence. God created all of us for Himself to be with Him forever. Men look to religion for the answers to their profound questions about man and his existence.

2. From the beginning of Creation man had sensed something of the hidden power he knows must be the ultimate explanation of all things. Different religions have tried to respond to man's queries. Hinduism uses myths and philosophy to answer man. Hindus practice asceticism and meditation in their flight toward God. Buddhism teaches that by devout confidence man ascends to freedom and enlightment. Other religions follow similar routes. The Catholic Church accepts truth and holiness of these religions and sees reflections there of that Truth, Christ, Whom she proclaims as "the way, the truth and the life." The Church exhorts her children to do everything possible to cooperate with others in preserving all that is good in their religions and in their cultures.

3. The Church looks kindly upon Moslems who adore the one God, and who associate themselves with Abraham. They revere Christ, not as God, but as a prophet. They also honor Mary. They esteem the moral life, prayer, almsgiving, and fasting. We of this Council urge all to forget any past misunderstandings and work together toward justice, freedom, and peace in the world.

4. Searching into the mystery of the Church we recall that Christians and Jews share a common root: a spiritual ancestry in Abraham, whose call includes all believers in Christ. The patriarchs, Moses, and the prophets are the beginning of the Church's faith and her election by God; the exodus of the chosen people from bondage foreshadows her salvation.

The Church cannot forget that she received the Old Testament through the people with whom God chose to establish the Ancient Covenant. The Church recalls that Christ was born according to the flesh (cf. Rom. 9:4-5) from God's chosen people, as was His Mother, the Virgin Mary. The Church believes that Christ, by His Cross, reconciled Jews and gentiles making them both one in Himself.

From the Jewish people came the Apostles and early disciples who proclaimed Christ to the world. Although the Jewish people by and large did not believe in Christ and His Gospel, they still remain most dear to God because of their forefathers. There is a great spiritual heritage between Christians and Jews which we wish to further through mutual understanding and respect. May this be the fruit of biblical and theological studies and of brotherly dialogue.

What happened in Christ's passion and death can in no way be blamed on all Jews living at that time nor on those of today. For by His Cross Christ freely and lovingly underwent His passion and death because of the sins of all men that all might be saved.

Great care should be taken in preaching God's word and in catechetical instruction not to present the Jews as repudiated by God as if this view came from the Holy Scriptures. Motivated by the Gospel's spiritual love and remembering her common heritage with the Jews, the Church repudiates and deplores all persecutions of the Jews and displays of anti-semitism at any time and from any source.

5. The Church proclaims the Cross of Christ as the sign of God's all-embracing love and the source of every grace. We call upon Christian people to be at peace with all men and so truly be the children of their Father in heaven.

Decree on the Apostolate of the Laity

(Apostolicam Actuositatem,
November 18, 1965)

A paraphrase by
Rev. Harold B. Bumpus

Introduction

1. United in Council, we desire to intensify the apostolic activity of the People of God, and to this end we turn our thoughts to the Christian laity. The laity's role is indispensible to the Church and derives from the layman's very vocation as a Christian. The spontaneous and fruitful activity of the Church's earliest laymen indicates a zeal that must be broadened and intensified to meet modern-day circumstances. Advances in population, science, technology and communication have vastly enlarged the field of the lay apostolate, a field that is in great part open to the laity alone.

In many areas of human life men rightly see themselves as self sufficient and independent but are sometimes tempted to a serious departure from Christian ethics and morals. And in the many places where priests are few or deprived of free ministry, the Church could barely exist without the laity. In this Decree we describe the nature, character, variety, basic principles, and pastoral directives of the apostolic action of lay people. These directives will define the status of the laity in Church law.

CHAPTER I

The Vocation of Lay People to the Apostolate

2. Participation of the Laity in the Church's Mission.

The "apostolate" is defined as all activites whose aims are a) to spread Christ's kingdom to the Father's glory; b) to involve men in Christ's saving redemption, and c) to rightly relate the whole world to Christ. The Christian calling by its very nature is also a calling to the apostolate. The Apostles and their successors, the bishops, have been given Christ's office of teaching, sanctifying, and governing; the laity share the priestly, prophetic and, kingly office of Christ.

Foundations of the Lay Apostolate

3. The laymen's apostolic right and duty flow from their faithful, hopeful and loving union with Christ, established and nourished through the sacraments. The laity are assigned to the apostolate by the Lord Himself as a royal priestly people (1 Pt. 2:4-10). So that the Church and the world lovingly may be built up, the Holy Spirit freely gives the faithful special and varied gifts, or charisms. Any of the faithful graced with a special gift possesses the right, the duty, and the freedom to exercise it, but always under the wise guidance of their pastors for the upbuilding of the Church. In all, care must be taken not to extinguish the Spirit.

The Spirituality of Lay People

4. The success of the apostolate of lay people depends on their union with Christ, a union maintained by the spiritual helps common to all the faithful, especially by the liturgy. Lay people should strive through the continuous exercise of faith, hope, and love to permeate all of their activities, familial and occupational especially, with their Christian spirit. "Whatever you do whether in

speech or in action do it in the name of the Lord Jesus" (Col. 3:17).

Only the light of faith and meditation on the Word of God can enable us universally to find God, in whom "we live and move and have our being" (Acts 17:28); only thus can we always seek His will, see Christ in all men, make sound judgments on the true meaning and ultimate value of temporal realities. Those with such a faith live in the expectation of the revelation of the sons of God, mindful of the cross and resurrection of the Lord.

On life's pilgrimage they are hidden with Christ in God, are free from the bondage of riches, and are in search of the goods that last forever. Generously they give their all to extend God's kingdom and to make the Christian spirit a vital energizing force in the temporal sphere. In life's trials they draw courage from hope, convinced "the sufferings of the present to be as nothing compared with the glory to be revealed in us" (Rom. 8:18).

With God's love motivating them, they do good to all, especially their brothers in the faith (cf. Gal. 6:10), putting aside "everything vicious, everything deceitful; pretenses, jealousies, and disparaging remarks of any kind" (1 Pt. 2:1), in this way attracting men to Christ. Divine love, "poured out in our hearts through the Holy Spirit who has been given to us" (Rom. 5:5), enables lay people to express concretely the spirit of the Beatitudes. Following Jesus in His poverty, they are not depressed in want nor proud in plenty; imitating the humble Christ, they are not anxious for vain pretense (cf. Gal. 5:26). They seek rather to please God and not man, always ready to give up everything for Christ (cf. Mt. 5:10), mindful of the Lord's saying: "If a man wishes to come after me, he must deny his very self, take up his cross, and begin to follow in my footsteps" (Mt. 16:24). In Christian friendship, they afford mutual support in all needs.

This lay spirituality will take its particular character from the circumstances of one's state in life (married and familial, celibate, or widowed), from one's state of health and from one's professional and social activity. Every individual has received from God talents and gifts suitable to his circumstances. These should be cultivated. Laymen should make their own the spirituality proper to the Church-approved associations of which they are members. They should also hold in high regard professional competence, family, and civic sense, and the virtues related to social behavior such as honesty, justice, sincerity, courtesy, and moral courage; without them there is no true Christian life.

The perfect example of this apostolic spiritual life is the Blessed Virgin Mary, Queen of Apostles. While on earth her life was like that of any one else, filled with the labors and cares of the home. Always, however, she remained intimately united to her Son and cooperated in a wholly unique way in the Savior's work. And now that she is assumed into heaven, her motherly love keeps her attentive to her Son's brothers, still on pilgrimage amid the dangers and difficulties of life, until they arrive at the happiness of the fatherland. Everyone should have an authentic devotion to her and entrust his life to her motherly care.

CHAPTER II
Objectives

5. The laity exercise their apostolate in the temporal world as well as in the spiritual world. These worlds are distinct, yet very closely related. The lay person, while both believer and citizen of the world, has only one conscience, a Christian conscience, which should continually guide him temporally and spiritually.

The Work of Spreading the Gospel

6. The apostolate of each of the Church's members aims at communicating by word and action the message and grace of Christ. Lay people have countless opportunities for exercising the apostolate of evangelization and sanctification. The witness of a Christian life, and good works performed in a supernatural spirit, are effective in drawing men to the faith and to God; just as the Lord has said: "Your light must shine before men so that they may see goodness in your acts and give praise to your heavenly Father" (Mt. 5:16).

Today it is not enough that the laity merely lead a "good life"; rather true apostles seek opportunities to announce Christ to non-believers or strengthen in faith those who already believe. We earnestly exhort the laity to take a more vigorous role, each according to his gifts and knowledge and in union with the mind of the Church, in explaining and defending Christian principles and in applying Christian values to the pressing human and religious problems of our times.

The Renewal of the World of Man

7. The elements that make up the temporal world, such as progress in justice and peace, are not mere helps to man's last end, but have a God-given goodness and value of their own, when used properly by men guided by Christ as their Head. Throughout the course of history mankind has failed in thought and action to appreciate this divine-temporal world; our own day sees some people making man a kind of slave to science and technology, rather than their master. It is the work of the whole Church to form men able to establish the proper set of values in the temporal sphere and to direct it towards God through Christ.

Pastors must teach the principles and provide the spiritual helps necessary for the renewal of the temporal world, a renewal that laymen ought to take on themselves as their distinctive task. In this task Christian social action is outstanding.

Charitable Works and Social Aid

8. The greatest commandment is to love God with one's whole heart and one's neighbor as oneself (cf. Mt. 22:37-40). Christ has

made this commandment of love of neighbor His own and has enriched it with a new meaning: He willed Himself and His brothers to be the objects of this love, saying: "As often as you did it for one of my least brothers, you did it for me" (Mt. 25:40). In taking on human nature, He has united Himself with all humanity in a supernatural solidarity which makes of it one united family. He has made love the distinguishing mark of His disciples by the words: "This is how all will know you for my disciples: your love for one another" (Jn. 13:35).

In every age the characteristic mark of the Christian and of his Church is love, a love made visible in the alleviation of all kinds of human needs—especially those of the poor and the sick.

Because modern means of communication and transportation have made the world's peoples into a single family, charitable action today can and should reach all men and all needs. This obligation binds first and foremost the richer individuals and nations.

If this exercise of love is to be above all criticism, one should see in one's neighbor the image of God in which he has been created, and the image of Christ because whatever is offered to the needy is offered to Him. The liberty and dignity of the person aided must be respected with the greatest sensitivity. Purity of intention should not be sullied by any selfishness or desire to dominate. The commands of justice must first be satisfied; that which is already due in justice is not to be offered as a gift of love. The cause of evils, and not merely their symptoms, ought to disappear. The help contributed should be organized in such a way that recipients are gradually freed from their dependence on others and become self-supporting.

The laity should therefore highly respect and support private and public works of love and social-assistance operations, including those international in scope. By these means effective aid is brought to needy individuals and nations. The laity should cooperate in these efforts with all men of good will.

CHAPTER III
The Various Fields of the Apostolate

9. The chief fields of the apostolate open to the laity are: Church communities, the family, the young, the social environment, the national and international spheres. Women are taking an increasingly active role in all aspects of society, and it is very important that their participation in the various sectors of the Church's apostolate should likewise develop.

Church Communities

10. The action of lay people within the Church communities is so necessary that without it the apostolate of the pastors will often be unable to reach its full effect. Following in the footsteps of the men and women who assisted Paul in the proclamation of the Gospel (cf. Acts 18:18-26, Rom. 16:3), lay persons with a genuine apostolic spirit meet

the needs of their brothers and are a consolation no less to the pastors than to others (cf. 1 Cor. 16:17-18). Nourished by participation in the liturgy, they eagerly contribute to apostolic works; they draw men towards the Church who had drifted away; they spread the Word of God especially by catechetical instruction. By contributing their competencies they increase the efficacy of the administration of all the Church's resources, spiritual and temporal.

The laity not only should work habitually in close union with their parish priests, but also should raise, discuss, and solve personal, theological, and international questions. According to their competencies, the laity should contribute to all the apostolic and missionary enterprises of their local parishes and dioceses.

The Family

11. The apostolate of married persons and of families has a special importance for both Church and civil society. The Christian marriage commitment gives couples responsibilities: to witness their faith to each other, to educate their children in it, and to offer to them wise guidance in choosing a vocation and a style of life.

To offer proof in their lives of the indissolubility and holiness of the marriage bond, to assert vigorously the right and duty of parents and guardians to give their children a Christian upbringing, to defend the dignity and rights of the family have always been the duty of married persons. Today, however, this has become the most important aspect of their apostolate. Christians must see that these rights are completely safeguarded in civil legislation and social administration involving housing, education, working conditions, taxation, retirement, and immigration regulations.

God Himself has commissioned the family as the primary cell of society. To fulfill this mission, affectionately and prayerfully the family must be a sanctuary of the Church; must share in liturgical worship; must practice justice and other good works towards all its needy brothers and sisters. The Christian family apostolate includes the following works, among others: adopting abandoned children, welcoming strangers with love, helping in the administration of schools, offering adolescents help and advice, helping engaged couples prepare for marriage, teaching catechism, giving material and moral support to married people and families in crisis, and procuring for the aged a just share of the fruits of economic progress that is above the survival level.

The example of Christian marriage and family life is especially important in regions where the Church is not firmly established. In these regions especially, the goals of the apostolate can more easily be realized when Christian families organize into small groups.

Young People

12. A complete transformation has occurred in young people. Their lifestyle, thought patterns, family relationships, social

and political values have all changed, giving them new responsibilities, social and apostolic. If the exuberant and energetic enthusiasm which is naturally theirs is penetrated by the Spirit of Christ and animated by a sense of obedience and love toward the Church's pastors, a rich yield can be expected from it. As young people grow gracefully independent, they must minister Christ to one another.

Adults and young people should share the personal riches that are mutually valuable to each other. The good example, advice and aid of adults will motivate young people to be apostles for Christ and win from them their respect, confidence, and esteem.

Children, too, in their own measure, are true living witnesses to Christ among their companions.

The Apostolate of Like Towards Like

13. It is the characteristic work and responsibility of lay people—they alone are capable of it—to infuse the Christian spirit into the mentality, behavior, laws, and structures of the communities. This is done by a balance of faith and action, by a righteousness that attracts people to Christ and His Church, by a charity that motivates lay people to share the burdens and aspirations of their brothers thus preparing all hearts for salvation, and finally by responsible fulfillment of their various duties with Christian generosity.

Genuine apostles will go further still and by their words reveal Christ to those around them, knowing that many will acknowledge Christ only if He is presented by the laymen with whom they associate.

The National and International Levels

14. In fulfilling their civic duties, Catholic lay persons will further a civil authority justly exercised and laws in accord with morality and the common good. Catholics whose political skill is balanced by a solid knowledge of Christianity should not decline public office.

With courteous understanding and in cooperation with all men of good intention, Catholics must seek means to improve the alignment of social and public institutions with the Gospel. Lay apostles must develop a sense of the solidarity of all peoples and indeed transform this sense into a desire for brotherly union. A sense of the theoretical and practical problems and solutions posed in the international sphere is also important, especially when these concern newly-developing nations. International relations should manifest a fraternal and mutual give-and-take; and international travelers should always and everywhere behave as the messengers of Christ that they are.

CHAPTER IV

The Different Forms of the Apostolate

15. The laity can exercise their apostolate either singly or grouped in various communities or associations.

Individual Apostolate

16. Nothing can replace the apostolate of the individual as the pre-requisite and the starting point of all types of lay apostolate. The individual apostolate has always been present, and sometimes is the only form of the apostolate appropriate or even possible. Every lay person, regardless of his circumstances, has the vocation and the duty to exercise his individual apostolate, even if he has not the opportunity or possibility of collaborating in associations.

Appropriate to our times and a manifestation of Christ alive in His people are their very lives when these witness to the higher motives of faith, hope, and charity. Also appropriate and sometimes necessary is the lay apostolate whereby each, to the best of his or her abilities and conditions, faithfully proclaims the Good News of Jesus the Christ in words, in works, and even in motives. All should recall that in public worship and by prayer, by penance, and by the willing acceptance of the labors and burdens of life in which they resemble the suffering Christ (cf. 2 Cor. 4:10; Col. 1:24), they can touch all men and thus contribute to the salvation of the whole world.

The Individual Apostolate in Certain Circumstances

17. We give God deeply-felt gratitude that in places under persecution He is raising up laymen who, with heroic courage, assume

partially the priestly responsibilities of teaching and exhorting those around them. Where Catholics are few and scatttered, the individual lay apostolate is very appropriate; for by facilitating friendships and discussions, the difficulties of isolation are lessened, the fruits of the apostolate increased, and witness given to the love engendered in the Church community.

Group Apostolate

18. Man is social by nature and God molds His faithful ones into a people of His own. Thus does the natural and the supernatural achieve a happy harmony in the apostolate of groups, which through their unity in Him witness to Christ's presence in the world. This group apostolate is seen in families, parishes, dioceses, and some free associations. Organizations created for the group apostolate, through their support, training, assignments, and directions promote much greater achievements than do isolated efforts by individuals. Such organizations, wherever they exist, vitally need increased strength in order to produce comprehensive and lasting results. They must be strong especially in their knowledge of the persons they serve, whose attitudes and social conditions are buffeted constantly by public opinion and social institutions.

Various Types of Group Apostolate

19. Those apostolic organizations are best which help the faithful tie together their life of faith with their life of everyday con-

cerns. The universality of the Church's mission requires that all individual members and organizations evermore perfectly unite and conform themselves to the Church's world-wide aims and concerns. Wasteful practices such as the following must be avoided: creation of new works without sufficient cause; antiquated works or methods prolonged; and the indiscriminate transfer of projects or methods from one country to others. Adherence to these norms and to ecclesiastical lines of authority insures the rights of the laity to establish, join, and direct associations for the lay apostolate.

Catholic Action

20. For decades now and in many countries, lay people have formed various societies which, in union with the hierarchy, pursue apostolic goals. Though these institutions use differing methods, they nonetheless yield abundant fruit and have thus earned praise and support from the bishops. These groups have been given the name of Catholic Action, usually have been described as a collaboration of the laity in the apostolate of the clergy and are constituted by a combination of all of the following characteristics:

a) Their immediate end is that of the Church; the evangelization, and sanctification of men and the Christian formation of their conscience, so as to enable them to permeate with the Gospel spirit the various social groups and environments.

b) The laity, in cooperation with the hierarchy, contribute their competence and assume responsibility in the direction of these organizations, in the investigation of the circumstances in which the Church's pastoral work is to be done, and in the formulation and execution of their plan of action.

c) The laity act with the unity of a living body, displaying the Church as a community and making the apostolate more fruitful.

d) The laity, either on their own initiative or in response to an invitation from their pastors, act under the direction of the hierarchy, which can give this apostolate an official standing.

When the hierarchy judges that organizations combine all these elements, they should regard them as Catholic Action, even though forms and names may differ according to locality and culture.

The Council most earnestly commends those associations which meet the requirements of the Church's apostolate in many countries; it asks the priests and laymen laboring in them to develop more and more the characteristics described above.

Special Commendation

21. Those associations which the hierarchy has praised, commended, and decided to found, as more vital to meet the needs of times and places, should be most highly valued by priests, religious, and lay people.

22. Special recognition is due to the laity who put themselves and their abilities at the service of the Church's institutions. The growing number of these lay persons is a great joy to the Church, especially when

they serve the Catholic communities in the missions and the younger churches. The appropriate response to the laity by pastors is joy and gratitude in providing them with spiritual comfort, encouragement, training, and the resources necessary for the maintenance of just and equitable living conditions for themselves and their families.

CHAPTER V

The Order To Be Observed

23. The lay apostolate truly belongs to the apostolate of the whole Church and needs to work in harmony with the hierarchy. This responsible collaboration will insure an effective witness to fraternal charity, the attainment of common ends, and the avoidance of ruinous rivalries.

Relations with the Hierarchy

24. The hierarchy's responsibility is to favor the lay apostolate, supply it with principles and spiritual assistance, direct the exercise of the apostolate to the common good of the Church, and see to it that doctrine and order are protected.

Yet this lay apostolate allows various kinds of relations with the hierarchy according to the different forms and goals of this apostolate.

For very many apostolic projects owe their origins to the free choice of the laity and their continued existence to the laity's skill in directing them. These projects sometimes advance the Church's mission and are thus praised by the hierarchy. The name Catholic is reserved, however, to those projects which enjoy the approval of Church authority.

There are forms of the lay apostolate which the hierarchy considers so closely united to its own spiritual purpose that it exercises a special responsibility for them. In doing so the hierarchy does not alter the special nature of a lay apostolate nor deny the laity their rightful freedom to act on their own initiative. This act of the hierarchy has been given the name of "mandate" in various Church documents.

The hierarchy and pastors also share with the laity some of their own duties: catechetical instruction, liturgical functions, and the care of souls. In these delegated duties, the laity are completely subject to directives of the hierarchy.

As for works and institutions of the temporal world, the hierarchy is responsible for teaching and interpreting the relevant moral principles. It is also their duty to judge, after mature reflection and with the advice of competent persons, how well such activities and institutions conform to moral principles and also to judge what is required to protect and promote the values of the supernatural order.

Relations with the Clergy and with Religious

25. Bishops, parish and other priests will recall that the rights and duties of exercising the apostolate are shared by all the

faithful, cleric and lay. For this reason they will work with and have a special concern for laity involved in apostolic works.

Priests with the necessary ability and training will be chosen to represent the hierarchy in helping special forms of the lay apostolate. In union with the Church they will a) promote good hierarchy-laity relations; b) foster the spiritual life and apostolic sense of the associations entrusted to them; c) offer advice and encouragement to them; d) with the laity seek out paths to a greater harvest; and e) develop the spirit of unity within the association and between it and others. These priests will be supported and assisted by Religious brothers and sisters who, with high regard for the lay apostolate, will gladly promote them as the spirit and rule of their Institutes permit.

Special Councils

26. Diocesan councils with clerical, Religious, and lay members should be established to assist the Church's apostolic endeavors. These councils can coordinate the various lay associations and preserve the freedom and identity of each. Such councils also should be established, if possible, on parochial, interdiocesan, national and international levels.

A special secretariate should be established at the Vatican a) to promote the lay apostolate; b) to supply information about the various apostolic initiatives of the laity; c) to research problems in this apostolate; and d) to assist the hierarchy and the laity in this apostolate. The various apostolic movements and associations of the lay apostolate the world over should be represented in this secretariate, which should have clerics and Religious available for collaborative efforts.

Cooperation with Other Christians and Non-Christians

27. The shared inheritance of the Gospel and the equally shared and consequent duty of giving Christian witness make it desirable, and often necessary, that Catholics cooperate with other Christians, either in activities or in societies; this collaboration is carried on by individuals and by religious bodies, and at national and international levels. Often human values shared by all mankind require of Christians working for apostolic goals that they cooperate with those who do not profess Christianity but acknowledge these values. Through this dynamic, yet prudent, collaboration, so important to activities in the world the laity witness to Christ the Savior of the World, and to the unity of the human family.

CHAPTER VI

Training for the Apostolate

The Need for Training

28. Training for the lay apostolate is required a) for the layman's progress in spiritual life and understanding of the Church's

teaching; b) to adapt themselves to the variety of situations, persons, and duties encountered in this apostolate; and c) to cement lay apostles in the educational foundations established by this Council.

Principles of Training

29. Required for effective efforts in the lay apostolate are the following:

a) a personalized, integrating, humanistic education;

b) personal adaptation into one's own society and culture;

c) knowledge of means to accomplish the mission of Christ and the Church;

d) solid grounding in theology, ethics, and philosophy;

e) appropriate practical and technical training;

f) the ability to live, work, and dialogue in a friendly fashion with others;

g) the patient prudence necessary to see oneself and all things in the light of faith; and

h) a lifestyle adjusted to an active service of the Church.

With these qualities and preparations, the laity can bring the Church's active presence into the very heart of the world.

Those Who Train Others for the Apostolate

30. Preparation for and adaptation to the apostolate is a life-long process, and those responsible for the various stages of Christian

education are also responsible for this apostolic formation.

By word and example parents and older family members must teach children concern for their neighbors' needs, material and spiritual. The larger family of the parish and its priests by their teaching, preaching, counseling, and other actions should foster an awareness of the apostolate of the People of God.

Catholic educational institutions and all others responsible for the education of Catholics should foster in the young a catholic outlook and apostolic action.

The various lay apostolic groups and associations rightly and frequently are the ordinary channel of doctrinal, spiritual, and practical training. This training should be pursued so as to extend beyond the activities of the associations themselves into all sectors of life, the professional and social sectors especially.

In fact, every lay person, proportionate to the awareness he has of his God-given talents and charisms, should endeavor evermore to better his apostolic service of his brothers.

Fields Calling for Specialized Training

31. Some types of apostolates require a method of training specific to themselves:

a) When the apostolate is that of proclaiming the Gospel and sanctifying men, the laity must be trained in dialoguing with believers and non-believers alike and in giving the witness of the Gospel to a world rampant with materialism.

b) When the apostolate is that of renewing the temporal world, the laity should be so instructed and experienced in the true meaning and value of temporal goods, in the organization of Christian social institutions, and in the Church's moral and social teaching that they can both further that teaching and apply it to concrete, individual cases; and

c) When the work is of charity and mercy, the laity must learn even from childhood how to sympathize with their brothers and to offer generous help in their time of need.

Aids to Training

32. The laity involved in the apostolate have available to them numerous aids that enable them to grow in their knowledge of sacred scripture and Catholic doctrine, to be nourished in the spiritual life, and to be appraised of world conditions and apostolic methods.

These aids and the centers and institutes which develop and promote them are mindful of the varying conditions under which the apostolate is exercised and thus have yielded excellent results. Programs of this kind are a joy to the Church and should be furthered in the regions that need them.

Centers of documentation and research should be established in theology, anthropology, psychology, sociology, and methodology for the benefit of areas of the apostolate.

Such centers create an atmosphere more conducive to developing the talents of the laity, men and women, young and mature.

Exhortation

33. We, the Council Fathers, earnestly entreat the laity, especially the young, willingly, nobly, and enthusiastically to respond to Christ's call and to the urging of the Holy Spirit. It is the Lord Himself, through this Council, who is inviting all the laity to unite themselves to Him ever more intimately, to consider His concerns as their own (cf. Lk. 10:1). It is the Lord Himself who calls the laity to the Church's apostolate, an apostolate that is a true unity of different forms and methods, an apostolate that must continually be adapting itself to the needs of the moment, an apostolate where the laity will show themselves His fellow workers, always doing their full share in the work of the Lord, certain in the Lord that their labor cannot be in vain (cf. 1 Cor. 15:58).

Decree on the Church's Missionary Activity

(Ad Gentes, December 7, 1965)

A paraphrase by
Rev. Simon E. Smith, S.J.

Preface

1. The Church has been sent by God to all nations to be the universal sacrament of salvation. So it tries to proclaim the Gospel to all people so that God's kingdom can be everywhere proclaimed and established.

Humanity is now moving into a new stage and this makes it more urgent to save and renew every creature and thus build up one family and one people.

CHAPTER I

Doctrinal Principles

2. The pilgrim Church is missionary by its very nature. It shares in the mission of the Son of God and of His Holy Spirit to mold all individuals into a people in which God's children can be gathered together.

3. In order to establish communion between sinful human beings and Himself and to mold them into a fraternal community, God intervened in human history by sending His Son, made man, to snatch us from sin and reconcile us to Himself. Moreover God appointed Him heir of all things, so that in the Son He might restore all things (cf. Eph. 1:10).

Jesus was sent into the world as a real mediator between God and humans. In His human nature He is the New Adam, the head of a renewed humanity. He became poor for our sakes so as to enrich us. He came to serve and to give His life for all. He took on our entire human nature in all its misery and poverty, though not our sin. What He once preached must be proclaimed to the ends of the earth so that what He once accomplished for the salvation of all may achieve its effect in all.

4. To do this, Christ sent the Holy Spirit to impel the Church to expand. He came on the day of Pentecost to remain with us forever. On that day the Church was publicly revealed to all, the Gospel began to spread among the nations by means of preaching, and finally there occurred a hint of the union of all peoples in a universal faith. That union is to be achieved by the Church which speaks, understands, and accepts all tongues. This Holy Spirit gives the Church unity in fellowship and in service. He acts as the soul of the Church and gives the faithful the same mission spirit which motivated Christ Himself.

5. Right from the beginning Jesus chose twelve men and sent them forth to preach. Actually they were the beginning of a sacred hierarchy. Again, after His death and resurrection, He founded His Church as the sacrament of salvation and sent His Apostles into all the world with the command: "Go, therefore, and make disciples of all the nations. Baptize them in the name of the Father, and of the Son, and of the Holy Spirit. Teach them to carry out everything I have commanded you" (Mt. 28:19). "Go into the whole world and proclaim the good news to all creation. The man who believes in it and accepts baptism will be saved, the man who refuses to believe in it will be condemned" (Mk. 16:15).

The mission of the Church is fulfilled by that activity which makes it fully present to all people and nations. By the example of its life and preaching, by the sacraments and other means of grace, it can lead all to the faith, the freedom, and the peace of Christ. This mission goes on forever. Following the example of the Apostles, the Church must walk the same road Christ walked: a road of poverty and obedience, of service and self-sacrifice to the death. From that death the Lord came forth a victor by His resurrection.

6. This duty, shared by the whole Church under the leadership of Pope and bishops, is carried out in a variety of ways. Usually it means preaching the Gospel (evangelizing) wherever God's word has not been heard, planting the Church and helping it grow until it can stand on its own. This naturally includes Baptism and the Eucharist and eventually the missionary activity of the young churches themselves. But where the Gospel cannot be preached, missionaries can still give witness to Christ by charity and works of mercy.

There is a real difference between missionary activity among the faithful and also efforts aimed at restoring Christian unity. Nevertheless these two latter activities are very closely connected with the Church's missionary goal, because division among Christians damages the life-giving work of preaching the Gospel to every creature and deprives many people of access to the faith. The same command which makes us a missionary Church calls all who are baptized to come together as one flock and to bear unanimous witness before all nations to Christ their Lord.

7. Such missionary activity flows from God's will and the need of the Church to share the love which is its own life for the glory of God until all people can say together with Christ, "Our Father."

8. In addition, missionary activity is very tied up with human nature and human hopes. Helping people know Christ is a service which helps them know themselves better and free themselves from sin for the service of others. The Church so transcends every distinction of race and nationality that she cannot be considered foreign anywhere or to anybody.

The words of Christ are at the same time words of judgment and of grace, of death and of life. For only by putting to death what is old are we enabled to come to a newness of life. This is as true of the goods of the earth as it is of persons, for "all have sinned and are deprived of the glory of God" (Rom. 3:23). Thus no one can claim on his own power freedom from sin or servitude. All need Christ, the Model, the Savior, and the Source of life. Indeed the Gospel has proved itself a force for progress in human history, a progress in liberty, brotherhood, and peace.

9. The time for missionary activity extends from the first coming of our Lord Jesus Christ until His second coming in glory. It is nothing more or less than the carrying out of God's will to make all people into one human community. The presence of Christ in the world, by preaching and sacraments, perfects the good already present in human hearts. It looks toward the time of fulfillment when Christ will come again.

CHAPTER II
Mission Work Itself

10. The task is enormous: billions of people have never heard the Gospel. Some of them belong to the world's great religions; others know no god; others deny the existence of God. So the Church must become part of these groups for the same reason Christ became like those among whom He lived.

Article 1: Christian Witness

11. All Christians have a duty to give good example so that other people can see the real meaning of human life and what unites humanity in community.

Hence Christians should join in the cultural and social life of the people among whom they live. They should know local, national and religious traditions. They should not let people lose a sense of divine things but help them to struggle for God's truth and charity.

They should respectfully learn by dialogue with other peoples what treasures God has given to all people and try to let the light of the Gospel shine on all.

12. Christian charity is not selective. It reaches out to all, of whatever race, social condition or religion they may be. The only Christian preference is for the poor and the oppressed and those who search for peace.

One special service to others which Christians should offer is education, in order to increase human dignity and prepare for more humane lives. And Christians should also struggle with people fighting famine, ignorance, and disease, in union with public, private, governmental, and international agencies of any religion.

All of this witnessing is not for the sake of material progress and prosperity but for more human dignity and community open to God in love.

Article 2: Preaching the Gospel and Gathering God's People Together

13. The Gospel is to be preached to all people so that they may believe and be converted. Conversion is the beginning of a spiritual journey which involves a change in outlook, morals, and social behavior. The Church forbids forced conversions and also insists on a person's right to believe in God.

14. After conversion there is a time of growth and training in the Christian life (called the "catechumenate") leading up to Baptism. This growth is the care of the whole Christian community which helps the new Christian to increase in faith, hope, and charity.

Article 3: Forming the Christian Community

15. The missionaries should try to form communities of Christians which will be signs of God's presence in the world. Nourished on God's word and the Eucharist, let them bear witness to Christ, walking in love and glowing with an apostolic spirit.

Such Christian communities should be self-reliant and deeply rooted among the people. They should have strong family lives, schools, associations for lay apostolates and open, sharing attitudes with those of other faiths.

Let them share, insofar as possible, in common profession of faith with other Christians and join in social, technical, cultural and religious projects, following the honorable customs of their own nation, avoiding any racism and nationalism, fostering instead a universal love for man.

The greatest importance here is with the lay people who should be involved in civic and cultural activities at every level. For this reason a variety of ministries is needed.

16. Vocations to the priesthood should be encouraged from among these communities and the training for the priesthood must firmly unite spiritual, doctrinal, and pastoral formation leading to complete dedication to the Church at all levels.

The whole training of students for the priesthood should be in the light of the mystery of salvation revealed in the Scriptures, lived out in the liturgy, and combined with every effort to become thoroughly familiar with the ways of thinking and acting characteristic of their own people.

For this reason such preparatory studies should be done while living and associating with their own people. Also, let the order of permanent diaconate be restored.

17. The role of catechists is of maximum importance. Hence they need thorough training and adaptation to cultural advances. Catechetical schools should be increased, refresher courses for catechists should be

held regularly and full-time catechists should be paid a just salary to provide social security and a decent standard of living. Let the extraordinarily valuable work of catechists and their helpers be recognized by public ceremonies which will increase their prestige in the eyes of the people.

18. Vocations to the religious life should also be encouraged and made to conform to local values and ways of expression. This is particularly true of contemplative vocations.

CHAPTER III
Particular Churches

19. When a new Christian community, rooted in social life and adapted to the local culture, has a certain stability and firmness, a milestone has been reached. It can now grow on its own and develop under the guidance of its own bishops and priests. Growth must continue to maturity through the exercise of responsibility in Church and civil life.

Let the young churches preserve intimate communion with the universal Church without losing their local cultural traditions. Let the missionaries continue to provide support in personnel and material until these young churches can provide for themselves.

20. Since particular churches mirror the universal Church, they, too, are sent to the people living around them to be a sign of Christ both by their example and by their preaching.

Let the bishop especially be a sign of Christ by his thorough awareness of his people and their condition. Let the local priests of the young churches work with the foreign missionaries and even offer to go themselves on missionary work to other territories.

Bishops are urged to provide continuing education for their clergy and let them provide for training young men to become priests and religious, making special provision and adaptation for those who cannot adapt themselves to the peculiar forms which the Church has taken on there.

Communion of young churches with the universal Church advances to perfection when they themselves send out missionaries to other nations.

21. The greatest attention is to be paid to raising up a mature Christian laity for without that the Church is not yet fully alive and remains an imperfect sign of Christ. The laity belong both to the People of God and to civil society. Their main duty is to bear witness to Christ by their life and works. Hence they must know their own culture, heal it, preserve it, develop it in accordance with modern conditions and finally perfect it in Christ.

Let them live in unity and solidarity with their fellow countrymen and share their faith with them. Let the clergy really esteem the laity and help them grow in responsibility.

22. The word of God, like a seed, sprouts from the good ground, drawing its nourishment from that ground where it has been planted and then it bears fruit. Thus the young churches grow up and are nourished

on the riches of their local traditions. For this reason theological study must be encouraged in each major cultural area of the world to lead to better adaptation of the Christian life to the genius and dispositions of each culture.

CHAPTER IV
Missionaries

23. Every Christian has the obligation to do his or her part in spreading the faith. Nevertheless, Christ calls certain ones to become missionaries and raises up certain groups to take on the special task of preaching the Gospel at home or abroad. These souls have a special vocation to serve those who are far from Christ.

24. Total devotion to the work of the Gospel as a missionary can demand a lifetime of sacrifice. The missionary bears witness to the love of God by an evangelical life, in much patience, in long-suffering, in kindness, in open, real love. Obedience to Christ is the mark of the missionary. Hence bishops and superiors should provide constant support and renewal for missionaries.

25. Missionaries need special training in order to be and remain persevering, patient, strong, open, adaptable and sympathetic. This requires practice and testing, to become persons of deep faith and self-discipline, resourceful and zealous.

26. Thus training for missionaries should stress familiarity with the Scriptures and extensive study of the peoples, cultures, and religions of the world. Most important is the study of missiology, the science of missionary

activity. Both theory and practical exercises are essential. And this applies even to short-term missionaries.

Such preparatory studies should be completed in the land to which the missionaries will be sent, in order that they can learn better the history, social structures, customs, values, tradition, and languages of the people whom they are to serve. Some should specialize in missiology, and bishops in mission countries should have many experts available for the service of missionaries.

27. None of these tasks can be accomplished by one person alone, and so communities of missionaries have been formed and should eventually work in service to and under the determination of the local church for whatever tasks are for the common good.

CHAPTER V
Planning Missionary Activity

28. Cooperation of those who plant and those who water is essential for the building up of the Church.

29. The primary responsibility to proclaim the Gospel throughout the world belongs to the body of bishops. The office of the "Propagation of the Faith" should alone be the principal coordinator of global missionary work by its activity of promoting missionary vocations and reporting on the missions.

Let this office raise and distribute both missionaries and funds according to real needs in mission areas.

Let it work with the Secretariat for Promoting Christian Unity to foster collaborative missionary work in order to overcome the scandal of division.

This office must therefore be both an administrative instrument and an agency of dynamic direction, made up of representatives of all areas of the world, of bishops and religious and lay people, and with a permanent body of experts to serve its needs.

30. The bishop is the principal coordinator of the missionary activity at the local level. He should have a pastoral council made up of clergy, religious, and laity.

31. Conferences of bishops should pool their resources to found projects for the common good.

32. Religious orders and congregations and other similar associations should defer to the local bishop in everything concerning missionary activity itself and should draw up contracts to govern their mutual relations. To maintain harmonious and on-going relations, all must keep as their top goal the growth of the young church toward its own independence.

33. Similarly religious congregations working in the same territory should form conferences to coordinate their activities and improve collaboration both on the mission and at home.

34. Missionary training institutes should collaborate with experts in ethnology, linguistics, history and science of religions, sociology, etc.

CHAPTER VI
Missionary Cooperation

35. Since the whole Church is missionary, the work of spreading the Gospel is a duty of the whole People of God. Hence, everyone in the Church has a share in missionary work.

36. As members of the living Christ all are duty-bound to assist the growth of His Body. The first and most effective way to spread the faith is by leading a profoundly Christian life, in union with other Christian communities. Prayer and penance will generate missionary vocations and funds. Modern communications media should be used to help Christians know and respond to the human needs in mission countries as well as the present condition of the Church in the world.

37. Besides their concern for missionaries from their own dioceses, the faithful of a parish should extend support to some parish or diocese in mission lands.

38. A bishop's responsibility extends beyond his own diocese to the universal Church. So bishops should stimulate, promote, and direct work for the missions so that their whole diocese becomes missionary.

They should encourage the sick and oppressed to pray and offer penance for the missions; they should encourage vocations to missionary congregations of Religious as well as promoting the works of such congregations and especially papal mission societies.

In view of the great shortage of priests in mission territories, bishops should send some of their better priests to such areas after careful training and under coordination of the Conference of Bishops. These Conferences of Bishops have a real responsibility for sending money and personnel to the missions and should consider founding missionary institutes from among their own clergy. In addition, it is up to these Conferences to provide a Christian welcome and pastoral care for immigrants from mission lands.

39. All priests, as representatives of Christ, are consecrated to the service of missions; so they should organize their pastoral activity to help spread the Gospel among non-Christians.

Hence by every means available to them priests should encourage zeal for the evangelization of the world. In seminaries let professors bring a missionary awareness to whatever they teach.

40. This Synod acknowledges the great work of both active and contemplative Religious communities in the evangelization of the world and urges them to continue untiringly in this work. As witnesses to the love of God and human community in Christ, contemplative communities have great importance and should found houses in mission areas. Active communities should re-assess their own priorities to decide whether they might not devote more energies to the missions. Secular institutes, too, can be of great help to the missions.

41. Lay people cooperate in the work of evangelization. As both witnesses and living instruments they share in the Church's

mission. In Christian countries they do this by encouraging knowledge, love, and support of the missions. But in mission lands let lay people (whether native or foreign) teach, administer, coordinate, organize, and promote various lay apostolates.

Lay people should offer socio-economic cooperation to developing countries. Special praise is due those lay people who work in universities or in historical and scientific-religious research promoting knowledge of peoples and of religions. They should cooperate with Christians, non-Christians, and international organizations. To help them in these tasks, they should be given technical and spiritual preparation in institutes established for this purpose.

Conclusion

We, the Council Fathers, together with the Pope, salute all missionaries, especially those who suffer persecution for the name of Christ. We pray God through the aid of the Virgin Mary, Queen of our Apostles that all nations may be led to the knowledge of truth as soon as possible.

Decree on the Bishops' Pastoral Office in the Church

(Christus Dominus, October 28, 1965)

A paraphrase by
Rev. Gregory J. Andrews

Preface

1. Christ our Lord was sent from God to forgive sins and to make all people holy. He in turn sent His Apostles, filled with the Holy Spirit, to continue His work of salvation through the Church.

2. In God's plan, the Pope, as the successor of Peter, holds a primacy of authority over the whole Church, just as Peter did. With the Pope, bishops, as successors of the Apostles, continue the work of Christ and His Apostles in history. Enlightened by the Holy Spirit, bishops are the authentic teachers of the Christian faith. In union with the Pope, they teach and govern the whole Church as shepherds.

3. Each bishop is entrusted with the care of a particular local church. The aim and scope of this pastoral office is the subject of this present decree.

CHAPTER I

Bishops and the Church All Over the World

I. The Role of Bishops

4. The bishops of the world together form a college or body headed by the Pope in which the authority of the Apostles over the whole Church is continued. An ecumenical council is a solemn meeting of the college of bishops acting in union with the Pope.

5.-6. Bishops share in responsibility for the whole Church. Their common concern should be for all the local churches, especially where the Word of God has not yet been heard, where there are few priests, and where the faith is in danger of being lost.

Bishops should encourage the Christian people to help and support the missionary activity of the Church. They should prepare and send priests and other workers wherever they are needed for this task.

Bishops should be mutually concerned for all the local churches or dioceses which make up the one Church of Christ. They should be willing to share their resources and to relieve the needs of areas afflicted by disasters.

7. Through their prayers and good works, they should unite themselves especially with their brother bishops who are under persecution or imprisonment for the sake of Christ.

II. The Pope and the Bishops

8. There can be no conflict between the special authority of the Pope over the whole Church and the proper authority of each bishop over the particular local church entrusted to his care. Ordinarily, a bishop may grant dispensations or special permissions to serve the spiritual welfare of the people in his own diocese.

9. The Pope is assisted by various central administrative offices of the Roman Curia, made up of Cardinals, bishops, priests, and laymen who act in his name and with his authority to serve the many local churches and their bishops. We wish these departments

to be reorganized and better adapted to the needs of the times.

10. Their members should be drawn from every part of the world to show the truly universal character of the Church. Diocesan bishops and lay people should especially be invited so that all may share appropriately in Church affairs.

CHAPTER II
Bishops and Their Local Churches

I. Diocesan Bishops

11. The whole Church is truly present in each diocese or local church. The care of particular churches is entrusted to individual bishops who are their pastors. With the cooperation of the priests in his diocese, each bishop teaches, governs, and makes his people holy as their chief shepherd in the name of the Lord.

Bishops should dedicate themselves fully to their task as witnesses of Christ before all people, not only those who already believe but also those who have strayed from the truth or have not heard the good news of Christ.

12. Preaching the Gospel and teaching the mystery of Christ are among the primary duties of bishops. They should show how the Church and the world are related in God's plan for salvation. Let them teach what the Church teaches about the freedom of the human person, marriage and family life, society, work and pleasure, science and art, poverty and wealth, social justice, war and peace, and the solidarity of the human family.

13. Bishops should preserve and teach Christian truth in a way which corresponds to the needs of the times, aware of contemporary problems with which their people must struggle. In doing so, they will show the loving concern of the Church for all people, especially the poor.

To carry out the mission of the Church in the modern world, bishops should be willing to engage in conversation with human society in a spirit of friendship and mutual trust. The message of salvation must be presented with the truth of simple language and the gentleness of understanding love. Every form of preaching and teaching and every medium of communications should be used to proclaim the Gospel of Christ.

14. Bishops should see to the proper instruction of all their people in the faith. According to their various needs and learning abilities, children, young people, and adults should learn about the traditions, the teachings, the life, and the worship of the Church. Good teachers must be provided for these tasks.

15. Appointed by God to make their people holy, bishops receive the full sacrament of Holy Orders, in which priests and deacons also have a share. They too minister to the People of God as their fellow workers.

Believing Christians have access to the mysteries of God through the bishop, their high priest. Bishops must therefore promote and oversee the worship of their local churches. By their preaching and prayers, they should never cease to help their people know and live the mystery of Christ's dying and rising through the Eucharist. Let their people be of one mind and form one body in Christ as the life and love of God grows within them through the sacraments.

Bishops should inspire everyone under their care by their personal charity and the example of a simple lifestyle. Through their efforts to lead their people to greater perfection and holiness and to foster vocations to the priesthood and religious communities, the true image of Christ's Church will shine forth brightly everywhere.

16. As pastor of his people, a bishop should stand in their midst as one who serves. Let him be a good shepherd and a true father who loves and cares greatly for everyone. Let him gather and mold all his people into one obedient family that truly lives and works together in love. For the sake of his people, he should arrange his life according to the needs of the times.

The bishop should look upon his priests as sons and friends, welcoming and listening to them with a trustful love, for they help him greatly every day to carry out his duties. He should be concerned for the holiness, the faithfulness, and the effectiveness of his priests as they live and work, providing retreats for them to renew their spiritual lives and holding meetings to bring their knowledge of the work of the Church in the modern world up to date. Priests who are in danger or who have failed in any way should be treated with patient, loving mercy.

From sociological surveys and by other means, a bishop must try to discover the true needs of his people in the circumstances in which they live. He must extend his pastoral care impartially to all his people, recognizing their duty and their right to work with him in building up and administering the Church.

He should work for the cause of religious unity, dealing with other Christian churches and non-Christian religions with great kindness and charity, and urging his people to do the same.

17. The bishop should give a unifying direction to all the organizations carrying out the work of the Church in his diocese. His people should be encouraged to join and support Catholic and Christian associations adapted to contemporary needs which pursue spiritual, charitable, and social goals.

18. Bishops should also be concerned for the spiritual welfare of those who cannot regularly be served by parish priests—exiles, refugees, migrant peoples, those who work on the sea and in the air, and foreign travelers. The bishops of each country should work together to meet the special needs of people in these circumstances.

19. In leading their people to salvation, bishops do not depend on civil authority in any way. They must be perfectly free in carrying out the mission of the Church. They will of course be concerned for the social and civil as well as spiritual progress of their people, so let them cooperate with public officials for these purposes and encourage their people to do the same.

20. We deeply appreciate the favorable attitude of many civil authorities toward the Church. We respectfully request, however,

that the privilege of appointing bishops be returned to its rightful place in the Church, wherever the custom has historically been otherwise.

21. When bishops are no longer fully able to carry out their urgent duties because of age or some other serious reason, they should be willing to resign. They will always be honored and supported by the Church.

II. Diocesan Boundaries

22. The whole Church must be clearly visible in each local church, and each bishop must be able to minister effectively to his people. For the good of the Church, the boundaries of dioceses should be revised. Wherever the welfare of the People of God may be served more perfectly, priests and the material resources of the Church should be redistributed reasonably and according to the needs of the many local churches.

23. Above all else, each diocese must operate with the organic unity of a properly functioning body. Civil boundaries and the special characteristics of regions and peoples should be taken into account in restructuring local churches. The size and population of each diocese should allow the bishop to perform his own proper duties adequately, to give direction to all the works of the Church going on within his diocese, and to know well the priests and people who help him carry them out. The area of the diocese should allow bishops and priests to devote all their energies to the service of their people without overlooking the needs of the Church all over the world.

Each diocese must have enough priests to care properly for God's people, sufficient offices and organizations to see to the works of the local church, and adequate resources for the support of diocesan personnel and institutions.

Bishops should also provide in some way for the spiritual needs of Catholics within their dioceses who belong to different Catholic traditions of the Church or who speak different languages.

24. The bishops of each country should work together to propose the most advantageous rearrangement of the boundaries and structures of dioceses within given provinces and regions of the Church.

III. Those Who Help the Diocesan Bishop

1. *Assistant Bishops: Coadjutor, Auxiliary*

25. In governing the local churches, the welfare of the People of God must always be the prime concern. Assistant bishops are often appointed to help the diocesan bishop carry out his pressing duties. Where a particular need exists such as the advanced age or ill health of the diocesan bishop, another bishop is sometimes appointed to assist him with the right to succeed him as bishop of the diocese at his death or retirement.

All assistant bishops must be given the authority which they need to work effectively within the diocese and to which they are entitled as bishops. Nothing must be taken away from the proper authority of the diocesan bishop.

The assistant bishops who share part of the burden of the diocesan bishop should be of one mind with him, and all should work in a spirit of mutual respect and brotherly love.

26. Whenever the welfare of his people will be served, a diocesan bishop should not hesitate to ask for bishops to be appointed to assist him, for they depend upon his authority. If something happens to the bishop of the of the diocese, one of his assistant bishops is usually given temporary charge of the diocese until a new diocesan bishop is named. To provide as far as possible for the present and future good of his diocese, the diocesan bishop should therefore consult with his assistant bishops on important matters, especially if one of them has been appointed with the right to succeed him as bishop of the diocese.

2. *The Administrative Staff of the Diocese: Curia and Council*

27. For the good of his diocese, the bishop may appoint several priests as his personal representatives who are given the authority to act in his name in certain matters or in certain parts of the diocese. Other priests constitute his senate or council and serve as consultants and advisors to the bishop, helping him in the government of the diocese.

The administrative staff of the diocese, made up of specially chosen priests and lay people, should be organized in keeping with present-day needs to serve as an effective instrument for the bishop in carrying out the work of Church in his diocese. We highly recommend that in each diocese the bishop establish and preside over a pastoral council to help him evaluate and make practical suggestions for the life of the local church.

3. Diocesan Priests

28. All the priests, both diocesan and religious within a diocese share with the bishop in the one priesthood of Christ. Diocesan priests dedicate themselves especially to the service of the local church to which they are attached. They form one priestly family with the diocesan bishop, who must be free to assign his priests as the good of the diocese demands. When a bishop and his priests are united by a bond of true charity and a common priestly will, the fruitfulness of their pastoral work will be increased. To this end, bishops should dialogue with their priests as a matter of course.

Diocesan priests should be commonly concerned for the spiritual welfare of their entire diocese and personally generous in contributing to its material needs.

29. We are especially grateful for the valuable service of priests who work in close cooperation with their bishop in schools and other institutions of the Church and among special groups of the Christian people.

30. As shepherds in their own right, pastors care for the People of God in the particular parishes of the diocese under the bishop's authority. Pastors and the priests

who assist them should work hard to make their people feel that they really belong to the community of the Church. Working together to do this, their pastoral work will become more effective. The priests and people of each parish should reach out with a missionary spirit to everyone living in their area. Priests should live together wherever possible as an example of charity and unity for their people.

Pastors have the duty to preach the Word of God to all Christian people so that they may grow as a community in the love of Christ. With the help of their own believing people, let them teach the mystery of salvation and true Christian doctrine to everyone and at every level of understanding.

Pastors should see that the Mass is at the center of the whole life of their parishes and that all their people receive the sacraments frequently, especially Penance, and participate actively in the worship of the Church.

Pastors must know their people well, especially the families, the young people, the poor and the sick, and the working people in their parishes. By visiting homes and schools and encouraging participation in the work of the local church, pastors will lead their people to holiness and help them to live truly Christian lives.

The priests who assist pastors contribute greatly to the welfare of their parishes. With a common purpose they should help and cooperate with their pastor and with each other as brothers in a spirit of mutual charity and respect.

31. The bishop should consider a priest's holiness, his knowledge of Christian truth,

and his enthusiasm for the work of the Church in entrusting him with the care of a parish. Since parishes exist only for the service of God's people, pastors are not in any way to be appointed on a competitive basis.

To assure stability and to better provide for the needs of the Christian people, the process of transferring pastors should be simplified. Those who are no longer able to carry out all their duties well should be willing to resign as pastors and will be supported by the bishop.

32. Motivated by true concern for the people of his diocese, the bishop may establish new parishes where they are needed.

4. Religious Communities

33. Priests, brothers, and sisters who belong to various Religious orders and congregations also cooperate in building up the Christian community. Let them always increase their dedication to the virtues of the Gospel, their prayers and sacrifices, the holiness of their lives, and their participation in the visible works of the Church in the world.

34. Priests who are members of Religious orders also truly belong to the diocese in which they work, in that they help greatly in serving the People of God and carrying out the work of the Church under the local bishop. Other men and women in Religious communities should increasingly help meet

the demanding needs of the Christian people, for they too belong in a special way to the diocesan family.

35. A common understanding of pastoral procedures is necessary within each diocese. Members of Religious orders should respectfully make themselves available to the diocesan bishop, for he may call upon them to assist him in the ministry of salvation, keeping in mind the particular character of their community. They should faithfully carry out his requests. At the same time however, those engaged in the works of the local church should always remain faithful to the spirit and the observances of their Religious congregations.

The authority of the diocesan bishop does not extend to the spiritual formation and internal affairs of Religious communities subject to the Pope alone for the service of the common good of the whole Church. Members of Religious orders are always responsible to the local bishop in such matters as pastoral care, public worship, preaching, and religious education.

Different Religious communities should cooperate closely with each other and with the priests who belong to the diocese in which they work. All should be united by charity in heart and mind for the good of the local church.

Bishops and the superiors of Religious communities should discuss together the nature of the pastoral work in which their priests are commonly involved.

CHAPTER III
Cooperation Among Bishops

I. National Conferences of Bishops

36. From the earliest days of the Church, local bishops worked together in a spirit of charity and fellowship, pooling their resources for the common good of their churches. They met together to establish a common pattern for teaching the faith and governing their churches. We wish to restore the ancient and honorable tradition of these meetings of bishops accordingly in our own times.

37. Today especially, bishops need to cooperate closely with one another to assure the success of the Church's work in the world, as conferences of bishops already established in many nations have proved. So that the common good of many local churches may be served, let bishops come together everywhere for the regular exchange of insights and experiences.

38. In these national conferences, bishops working together can more effectively promote the salvation which the Church offers mankind through special programs and offices adapted to the needs of the times and places.

Diocesan bishops, the bishops who assist them, and certain other bishops all share proportionately in the processes of consultation and voting, according to the working rules of the episcopal commissions they establish for themselves. Subject to approval by the Pope, their decisions have binding force.

Whether drawn from one or several nations, conferences of bishops should communicate with one another for the good of the Church in all parts of the world. Bishops assembled together from the ancient churches in the Eastern part of the world should take into account the common good of the different traditions of the Church which exist in their territory.

II. Provincial and Regional Boundaries

39. In view of various geographic and social conditions, the work of the Church is made more fruitful where several dioceses in the same area are established as a province. Relations among their individual bishops, with the archbishop of the province, and with civil authorities can thus be improved.

40. Therefore the existing boundaries of provinces are to be reviewed and the rights and privileges of their archbishops redefined. All dioceses not already attached to a province under an archbishop must become so or be formed into a new province. Several provinces should in turn be grouped into a regional unit of the Church.

41. Provincial and regional boundaries should be reviewed according to the same principles put forth for the revision of diocesan boundaries, before being submitted to the Pope for approval.

III. Special Offices

42. Certain new agencies will be established to serve many dioceses in particular regions or countries where the pastoral work of the Church must be carried out jointly. The personnel of these offices, diocesan bishops, and national conferences of bishops should always cooperate willingly for the good of the Christian people they mutually serve.

43. A special office for the spiritual care of military personnel should be established in each nation. The dedicated service of military chaplains should always be met with whatever assistance diocesan bishops can provide, especially priests qualified for this special work of the Church.

Conclusion

44. We wish finally the principles put forth in this document to be faithfully reflected in the code of Church law now being revised.

To help bishops and pastors to be even better shepherds of their people, directories providing guidelines for every form of pastoral care should be drawn up for their use. According to the needs of different regions and countries, directories for the spiritual care of special groups within the community of the Church and for the instruction of the Christian people in the truths of the faith should also be prepared.

Decree on the Life and Ministries of Priests

(Presbyterorum Ordinis, December 7, 1965)

A paraphrase by
Mr. Robert Gibbons

Introduction

1. All priests are assigned crucial and difficult tasks in the renewal and building up of Christ's Church on earth. Hence we seek to cultivate a fuller understanding and a deeper appreciation of the priest and his ministry and to explore ways of making that ministry more effective.

CHAPTER I
The Priesthood in the Church's Mission

Nature of the Priesthood

2. In Christ all faithful are made a holy and royal priesthood. All members have a part in the mission of the Church. The Lord Jesus established different offices for His people. Those members consecrated for the ministerial priesthood are marked with a special character; they are so configured to Christ that they can act in the person of Christ; thus through the ministry of the priest the whole body of the faithful is joined to the sacrifice of Christ, which is offered through his hands in the Eucharist.

As Christ, the High Priest, was sent by His Father to minister to men, He in turn sent forth His Apostles to act as priests, giving them the mission of ministering to men publicly in His name. Likewise, Christ made the successors of the Apostles, the bishops, sharers in this mission entrusted originally to the Apostles. This mission, this ministerial role, has been handed down to priests in a limited or lesser degree. Thus the priest serves as a co-worker of his bishop in the bishop's continuing fulfillment of the mission entrusted initially to the Apostles.

The duty of the Apostles and bishops in which the priest shares is this: to proclaim the Gospel of Christ, to unite the People of God, to promote the spiritual life of men, to continue the offering to the Father of the sacrifice of Christ and of ourselves, to pursue the glory of God.

Place of Priests in the World

3. The priest is taken from among men and appointed for men for things which pertain to God. He is set apart and is blessed with special graces not given to others. Yet this is not an end in itself. The priest is set apart from other men so that he will have the opportunity to be more totally dedicated to and immersed in his work of witnessing to men here and now of the divine. If he is to be an effective minister to men, the priest will have to be familiar with the life of men and the problems that life presents, while not falling into conformity to the world. He is called to act as the good shepherd who knows his sheep.

CHAPTER II
The Ministry of Priests

The Functions of Priests

Priests as Ministers of God's Word

4. Since no one can be saved who has not first heard and believed the Good News, the priest by his ordination and commission has the principal obligation of proclaiming the Gospel to all men by applying in word and deed its eternal truths to the events and realities men face in their daily lives. The Gospel, the Word of God, will plant the seed of faith in the unbeliever and nourish the faith of the believer. This process of strengthening faith through the proclamation of God's word is especially visible in the Liturgy of the Word during Mass. For there, in the Mass, the proclamation of the death and resurrection of the Lord is immediately joined to the response of the people as they join in the offering of Christ and themselves.

Priests as Ministers of the Sacraments and the Eucharist

5. God raises up men to be companions and helpers in the work of salvation. Thus, in addition to proclamation of the Gospel, the priest, as minister of Christ, is charged with performing sacred functions, particularly the administration of the sacraments.

Each sacrament contributes to the sanctification of the faithful. Of essential importance is the Eucharist, whereby one is fully joined to the Body of Christ. The priest should promote a better understanding of its significance and a prayerful participation by the laity in the Sacrifice of the Mass. The priest is to instruct the faithful to offer to God the Father in the Sacrifice of the Mass Jesus, the divine victim, and to join to that sacrifice the offering of their own lives.

The priest should urge the people to receive willingly the sacrament of penance. Further, he should seek to develop a spirit of prayer in the faithful that pervades all aspects of life.

Priests as Rulers of God's People

6. The priest is also intended to be a leader, drawing men together and guiding them through Christ to the Father. He should treat all as brothers and sisters, yet always remembering that he is simultaneously a father and shepherd. He should not fear reprimanding men for their failings, for he is charged with leading individuals to Christian maturity. He should reach out to all his flock, especially the poor and needy, youth and parents, beginners and religious.

The priest, especially the pastor, is also responsible for the formation of a living, dynamic Christian community, centered on the Eucharistic celebration. Such a community will foster a spirit of charity, prayer, and penance, not only for the local church, but also for the Universal Church. By its example the community will lead others to Christ and, at the same time, strengthen and nourish the faith of its members.

Priests' Relations with Others

Relation Between Bishops and the Priestly Body

7. The Bishop should recognize his priests as necessary and invaluable helpers and counselors, for the priests share in the same ministry and priesthood that he enjoys. Their priestly unity is symbolized in concelebration. The bishop should willingly listen to and consult with his brother priests. Such communication may effectively be advanced by establishing a priests' senate or similar representative group in each diocese. Finally, he should treat his priests as brothers and friends and be gravely concerned about their material and spiritual state.

For their part, priests should remember that it is their bishop who possesses the priesthood in all its fullness, that in him is vested the authority of Christ. The bishop bears the ultimate responsibility for the souls of the People of God. As sharers in that responsibility, priests ought to unite, in charity and obedience, with their bishop. No priest can fulfill his mission alone.

Brotherly Bond and Cooperation Among Priests

8. Though their duties vary widely, all priests are bound together in an intimate

sacramental brotherhood and share in the same mission. Their goal is the same, the building up of Christ's Church. It is of utmost importance that all priests, diocesan and religious, help each other in their ministries. On the personal level, priests should show a spirit of kindly fellowship among themselves and should display a special concern for the sick, lonely, overburdened, and wayward priests. To combat loneliness and its attendant dangers and to promote cooperation in their ministries, priests are urged to live some sort of community life; this can take many forms, depending upon the circumstances.

Relation of Priests with Lay People

9. The priest is a father to the faithful, their leader and guide. He must shepherd his flock, however, in the spirit of Christ, remembering that he is also a brother through Baptism and servant of his people. Priest and people should therefore seek together the things of Christ. The priest should listen to the laity and, recognizing the many talents of lay people, encourage them to use the talents God has given them to contribute to the building up of Christ's Church. The priest should labor to reconcile those who feel alien to the Church and its ways, those who have strayed, and those who have not yet been led into the Church. The faithful should love and honor their priests, follow them with love, and help them with willing prayer and labor.

The Distribution of Priests, Priestly Vocations

The Proper Distribution of Priests

10. Christ told the Apostles that their mission extended "to the very ends of the earth" (Acts 1:8). Hence, the mission of the priest is a universal one intended for all peoples at all times. Dioceses blessed with many priests should freely spread this wealth to those less fortunate. Rules for the transfer of priests from one diocese to another should be revised to correspond better to bishops' pastoral needs.

Priests sent to mission fields should not be sent alone, but rather at least in twos or threes. Priests who are sent to such fields should be familiar with the unique characteristics of their new flock, such as language and social customs.

Priests' Care for Priestly Vocations

11. All Catholics should cooperate through prayer or more active endeavors, to ensure an adequate supply of priests. Priests particularly should assist in fostering vocations. Priests, by spreading the Gospel and expressing in their lives a joyous Christ-like spirit, can do much to evidence both the importance and the rewards of the priesthood. Priests should remind the faithful often of the need of vocations and cultivate with great care the seeds of a priestly vocation when they see it.

CHAPTER III
The Life of Priests

Priests' Call to Perfection

Call of Priests to Holiness

12. At the baptismal font all believers are blessed with the grace to enable them, in spite of their human weakness, to reach for the perfection Christ intends for them. Priests particularly should strive for this perfection. But God, in the Sacrament of Orders, has given priests special graces to aid them in this quest.

13. A priest's service to others helps to make the priest more Christ-like; the ministry itself contributes to the increase of the priest's holiness. This increase in holiness in turn leads to a more effective and productive ministry.

We desire to achieve the pastoral goals of renewal within the Church: the spread of the Gospel throughout the world and dialogue with the modern world. Therefore we earnestly exhort all priests to use the appropriate means endorsed by the Church as they strive for that greater sanctity which will make them increasingly useful instruments in the service of all God's people.

Jesus gave Himself as a Victim to make men holy. As ministers of sacred realities, especially in the celebration of the Eucharist, priests represent the person of Christ in a special way and are likewise invited to give themselves for the sanctification of others. In offering the Eucharistic Sacrifice, the continuation of the work of our Redemption, the priest fulfills his chief duty. At the same time, in receiving Christ's Body and Blood, he is nourished by and shares in Christ's love. For these reasons, priests are strongly urged to celebrate Mass every day. Similar benefits accrue to the priest in administering the various other sacraments. As he becomes further involved in the love and work of Christ, he becomes close to Christ and as a consequence, becomes a better priest.

In nourishing the faithful, the priest should convey such a confidence in the faith that the hope of the people is aroused. The priest must always seek what is good for the faithful, not for himself, and always be ready to follow where the Spirit leads.

Unity and Harmony of Priests

14. In today's busy world, the priest often finds himself leading two unconnected, unrelated lives — the external life of the busy preacher and shepherd, and the internal life of the prayerful child of God and brother of Christ. In Christ he can find that union of the external and the internal, of the worldly life and the spiritual life. Christ gave Himself completely in service to mankind. By devoting himself to the service of men, by carrying out his priestly ministry, the priest is drawn closer to Christ, made more Christ-like, and thereby enters into a realm where every act

of his priestly ministry leads him ever closer to that spiritual perfection Christ desires for him.

Loyalty to Christ can never be divorced from loyalty to His Church. This requires that the priest always work in union with the bishop and with his brother priests. In this way a priest will find the unity of his own life in the very unity of the Church's mission.

Special Spiritual Requirements in the Life of the Priest

Humility and Obedience

15. Let the priest seek not his own will, but the will of Christ and follow it, in humility, wherever it leads. The Redemption was accomplished by a Son who was totally obedient to the Father. In imitating Christ's obedience, the priest becomes more Christ-like and thus better able to fulfill his ministry.

The priest's individual mission is but a part of the mission of the entire Church. Hence he should act in union with the Church and accept humbly the directions of the Pope, of his Bishop, and of his Superiors. He should expend all his energy in carrying out whatever task is assigned to him, no matter how lowly or unimportant it may seem.

Priestly obedience leads to real freedom. It opens the priest's heart to the will of Christ and frees him to give himself entirely to the service of Christ and His Church.

With singleness of purpose, he is to seek constantly new and better ways of serving the People of God. The priest should not fear making suggestions to his Superiors, but ought to be ready to submit to the decisions of those who bear the ultimate responsibility for the salvation of souls.

Celibacy To Be Embraced and Esteemed as a Gift

16. Perpetual continence was recommended by Christ for the sake of the kingdom of heaven. It is not demanded by the very nature of the priesthood, as is evident from the practice of the primitive Church and from the tradition in the Eastern Churches, where there exist married priests of outstanding merit. For reasons which are based in the mystery of Christ and His mission, celibacy was at first recommended to priests, and then in the Latin Church was imposed by law on all who were promoted to Sacred Orders.

Celibacy is both a valuable sign to the faithful and a significant aid to the priestly mission. It is a sign of that mysterious union and intimate relationship between Christ and His Church which exists here and now and will be fully manifested in the world to come. The celibate priest exhibits to men a total commitment to his priestly mission of service. Celibacy liberates the priest so that he may give himself completely to the service of God and all men. It allows him to unite with Christ with undivided heart.

Relation with the World and Worldly Goods: Voluntary Poverty.

17. The priest should appreciate created goods, for they are gifts from God. But the priest should develop a detachment from worldly goods and view them from the perspective of his priestly mission, using such materials in a manner that accords with God's will and promotes the priest's work.

The priest is urged to choose voluntary poverty. This will lead to the spirit of poverty endorsed by Christ, release the priest from the bonds of materialism, and serve as a living witness that his ultimate values are not those of this world. The priest may begin by sharing goods in common with his fellow priests. The priest and bishop should avoid all appearance of vanity and pretensiousness in their possessions and style of life, so that no one, rich or poor, may fear approaching them.

Helps for the Priest's Life

Helps Toward Fostering Interior Life

18. The priest advances toward Christlike perfection in fulfilling the roles associated with the public priesthood: proclaimer of the the Gospel, celebrant and administrator of the sacraments, leader of the faithful. In addition, the priest is aided in this quest for holiness by those means of sanctification available to

all men. Chief among these are Scripture and the Eucharist.

Reception of the sacraments, particularly Penance, will strengthen the priest's union with Christ. Daily meditation before the Blessed Sacrament, spiritual retreats, mental prayer, and spiritual direction are excellent means for leading the priest to a more pervasive spirituality. The priest should venerate the Mother of God, the Blessed Virgin Mary, using her as a model of the desired openness one should have to the Spirit.

Study and Pastoral Knowledge

19. A successful priestly ministry is greatly dependent on a mature knowledge of matters divine and human. The priest must be ready to answer the questions men pose and to converse effectively on current issues. The priest's search for deeper knowledge should continue throughout his life.

The development of the priest's knowledge should therefore center upon reading and meditation on the Sacred Scriptures. Sound familiarity with the writings of the Fathers and Doctors of the Church, especially with the documents expounded by the Popes and by the Councils of the Church, and with the work of the best of prudent theologians is also highly desirable.

Bishops should provide ways for their priests to attend courses in theology and pastoral methods. Such courses should be offered at set intervals and should encourage dedication to theological study.

The Provision of Just Remuneration for Priests

20. The faithful, for whom the priest labors, are genuinely obliged to ensure that fitting economic means are made available to the priest, so that he may lead a worthy and respectable life. The priest deserves a just recompense for his service. Bishops should make provisions for yearly vacations for their priests.

Common Funds To Be Set Up: Social Security for Priests To Be Organized

21. Common funds should be established and administered at diocesan or higher levels, to aid priests financially, to provide them with health care benefits, and to support aged and ill priests. When the priest is relieved of worry about his economic future, he is given freedom to devote himself more readily to the mission of salvation.

Conclusion and Exhortation

22. Priests are assigned difficult tasks, and this is particularly so in the present age when social customs and economic systems are rapidly changing, when long-held beliefs and values are increasingly questioned. Let priests turn away from feelings of ineffectiveness, loneliness and depression. Rather, let them view the world and its people as

God did and does — with overwhelming love. Let them see in the faithful those gifts and talents that enable them to become the building blocks of Christ's Church. Let them be mindful that they have as partners the priests and faithful of the whole world. If the world today requires that the Church approach it by new avenues, then we must be prepared to do so. Let priests always be ready to adapt their ministry to such changing conditions.

The plan of salvation is a mysterious one. It is revealed slowly. The Kingdom of God will spread only if the faith is deeply rooted in the hearts and minds of the faithful. Priests cannot and should not expect stunning victories in every endeavor. Let them be mindful, however, that Jesus has overcome the world (Jn. 16:33) and that the Gospel now bears fruit in many places through the work of the Holy Spirit.

For all their labors in the Kingdom of Christ, we affectionately offer our thanks to all the priests of the world: "To Him whose power now at work in us can do immeasurably more than we ask or imagine — to Him be glory in the Church and in Christ Jesus...(Eph. 3:20-21).

Decree on the Appropriate Renewal of the Religious Life

(Perfectae Caritatis, October 28, 1965)

A paraphrase by
Sister M. Jerome Leavy, O.S.B.
and Sister Mary Gregoria Rush, O.S.F.

1. In the Constitution on the Church we explained how the teaching and example of Jesus have always led certain men and women to live lives of poverty, chastity, and obedience. These people reveal to us some idea of the Kingdom of God by their dedicated lives. In this document we plan to consider the rules governing the lives of these Religious people and to make provision for their needs in our present world.

From the very infancy of the Church, there have existed men and women who strove to follow Christ more freely and imitate Him more nearly by the practice of the evangelical counsels. Each in his own way has led a life dedicated to God. Under the influence of the Holy Spirit, many of them pursued a solitary life, or founded Religious families to which the Church willingly gave the welcome and approval of her authority.

And so through the centuries a great variety of Religious communities and lifestyles developed. Each of these various gifts add to the life of the Church and make her more able to do what Jesus commanded her to do. However, all Religious persons devote themselves to the Lord in a special way and give themselves ever increasingly for Christ and for their fellow men who make up His Body, the Church. Therefore the more ardently they unite themselves to Christ, the more vigorous will be their Religious lives and the life of the Church.

A life consecrated by vows is valuable and necessary to the Church and the world in our present age. That this kind of life and its modern expression may achieve greater good for the Church, we issue the following decrees concerning the general principles to be used by the Religious themselves in appropriately renewing the life and rules of their communities.

2. Two processes are to be used together in renewal of Religious life: (1) a continuous study of the sources of the Christian life and the original inspiration of each community, and (2) its continuous adjustment to changing times.

Under the influence of the Holy Spirit and with the guidance of the Church the renewal of Religious life will follow the following principles:

1) The Gospel is the supreme law of all Religious life.

2) The particular gift and heritage of each community is to be preserved.

3) All communities should participate in the life of the Church, making her projects and goals their own.

4) Religious persons must become aware of the needs of people living in the modern world.

5) The basis of all renewal must be a renewal of spirit, an interior renewal of each individual Religious man and woman and of each community of Religious. Unless this spiritual renewal is accomplished all other attempts at renewal will fail.

3. We wish Religious communities to re-examine the rules, constitutions, customs, and structures which govern them in their manner of living, praying, and working. These should be adapted, in the light of the Decrees of this Council and the needs of contemporary

society, for forms which provide a lifestyle for the Religious person which is in harmony with the thinking of the Church and the concerns of the people of our time.

4. Each member of a Religious community is to be involved in the renewal of the life of the community. Following prudent experimentation allowed by church authority, final responsibility for renewal lies with the appropriate superiors. But fidelity to commitment to Christ expressed in a diligent living out of the principles of the Gospels by every Religious — such is the true hope of renewal. Therefore, in fidelity to their profession and in renunciation of all things for the sake of Christ, let them follow Him as their one necessity. Let them listen to His words and be preoccupied with His Work.

5. To this end, as they seek God before all things and only Him, the members of each community should combine contemplation with apostolic love. By the former they adhere to God in mind and heart; by the latter they strive to associate themselves with the redeeming work of Christ the Lord.

6. The Religious persons should accept every opportunity to develop their love of God and strengthen their life with Christ. We believe the dedication to life with Christ in God will lead to increased dedication to service of their neighbor. Members of Religious communities should then strengthen their life of prayer through daily meditation on the sacred writings and participation in the Sacrifice of the Mass as the center of their lives. They should strive through these means,

that is, the Eucharist and the Scriptures, to live and think with the Church and spend themselves on her mission to all men.

7. There are many unique Religious communities with a variety of gifts in the Church. Those Religious persons whose lives are totally dedicated to contemplation have a distinguished part to play in Christ's Mystical Body. Renewal of their manner of living should aim at keeping their practices of contemplative life at their holiest.

8. There are numerous clerical and lay communities in the Church—orders, congregations, societies of priests, brothers, and sisters engaged in teaching, retreats, parish work etc. The Church has assigned to these communities a special work of charity to be done in her name, and as a result their Religious life requires apostolic action and service.

For a Religious person to answer Christ's call and serve Him in His members, apostolic work must grow out of intimate union with Him and promote love for God and neighbor. Observances and practices in these communities should be arranged mindful of the needs of the apostolate. Since their religious life is committed to apostolic works in many different forms, diversity is required for appropriate renewal, and members will need to be sustained in living for Christ's service by proper means.

9. Monastic life in the East and West should remain and grow in its own authentic spirit, giving glory to God through divine worship in the hidden life and through apostolic works.

Renewal and adaptation in monasteries should be in keeping with the identity of each institution. Then they will become sources of growth for Christian people. Religious communities combining choral prayer and monastic observances are to keep that form of life in accord with their apostolate.

10. The lay Religious life, a state of total dedication to the evangelical counsels, is highly regarded by the Church. Its purpose is to carry out the work of the Church in education, caring for the sick, and other services.

Some brothers of Religious congregations can receive Holy Orders to provide priestly functions for their own houses, as long as the lay character of the congregation stays the same, and the decision is made by the General Chapter.

11. Closely related to Religious communities because of their dedication to chastity, poverty, and obedience are the Secular Institutes. Members of these communities must preserve their secular character so that they may exercise their proper ministry which is both in the world and, in a sense, of it.

12. All Religious persons profess vows of chastity, poverty, and obedience in order to live the counsels of Jesus given in the Gospels. Chastity practiced on behalf of the Kingdom of Heaven is a gift of grace which frees the heart of the Religious in a unique way for love of God and for all mankind. We urge all Religious to strive to live their vows faithfully by trusting in God's promised help, and to practice mortification and custody of the senses, and to take advantage of natural

helps to good physical and mental health. True fraternal love in communities and proper training in celibate living are strong helps to the Religious in living the vow of chastity.

13. Poverty voluntarily embraced in imitation of Christ provides a witness which is very valuable in today's world. A Religious person ought to be poor in fact and in spirit, sharing in the poverty of Christ. Religious communities also must give corporate witness to poverty by avoiding all appearance of luxury, of excessive wealth or accumulation of possessions.

14. Through the profession of obedience, the Religious offer to God a total dedication of their own wills as a sacrifice of themselves; they unite themselves with greater steadiness and security to the saving will of God. In a spirit of faith and of love for God's will, let all Religious show humble obedience to their superiors in accord with the norms of rule and constitutions. Knowing that they are giving service to Christ in the members of His Body, the Church, the Religious should carry out their tasks with all the resources of their minds and hearts, using all of their talents and gifts of nature and grace according to God's design expressed through their lawful superiors. Superiors in their turn should exercise their authority in a spirit of service for the members of the community. They should listen willingly to the Religious and encourage each to make a contribution to the welfare of the community and of the Church. Not to be weakened however is the superior's authority to make decisions about

what is to be done and to require obedience of the members of their communities.

15. A Religious community is a true family gathered together in the Lord's name and rejoicing in His presence. Community life in a Religious group should follow the example of the early Church gathered in Jerusalem. It should be prayerful and alive with charity for all members which is an overflow of the Holy Spirit poured into it by God. Religious families should examine those class distinctions which may exist in their communities and as far as possible see that they are abolished. All members should have equal rights and status except in cases where ordination to the priesthood confers unique distinction.

16. The enclosure or physical separation from the world of nuns totally dedicated to contemplation should be continued, but outdated customs related to it should be done away with. Sisters and other nuns devoted to external works need not be enclosed strictly but should maintain areas of privacy in their convents.

17. Since Religious habits are signs of a consecrated life, they should be simple and modest. They should meet the requirements of health and be suited to the situations and services required by those who wear them.

18. The renewal of Religious communities depends largely on the training of the members. The Religious persons should have several years of training in the life of the Religious community and proper professional education for the apostolic work which they will be asked to accomplish. Education should

contribute to the integrity of the life of the Religious and should be a continuous process throughout their lives leading to their spiritual, doctrinal, and professional development.

19. The establishment of new Religious communities should be done with serious thought. Where the Church has newly taken root, special attention should be given to the establishment and development of fresh forms of Religious life. These should take into account the natural endowments and the manners of the people, and also local customs and circumstances.

20. While existing communities remain faithful to their traditions, they will also be ready to adapt to the needs and culture of the people among whom they work.

21.-22. Through the approval and at the direction of the appropriate Church authorities some communities may join together for mutual support especially if they are small and share a common tradition. Some smaller communities may be absorbed into the larger; some may be disbanded, and some allowed to die out if the Church perceives they have little chance of flourishing.

23. Coordination of the efforts of all Religious communities can be achieved through conferences of major superiors established by papal authority.

24. Vocations to Religious life should be nurtured by priests in their parishes, teachers among their students, and especially by parents in their homes. The Religious themselves should not forget that the personal living of the vows can attract young persons

by its simplicity and authenticity to follow the call of Christ.

25. Religious communities for which these norms of renewal are decreed should react with a willing spirit to their divine calling and their contemporary mission in the Church. Let all Religious persons spread throughout the whole world the good news of Christ by the integrity of their faith, their love for God and neighbor, their devotion to the Cross, and their hope of future glory. Thus, with the aid of Mary, the Mother of God, "whose life is a rule of life for all," they will experience a daily growth and yield a harvest of fruits that bring salvation.

Decree on Priestly Formation

(Optatam Totius, October 28, 1965)

A paraphrase by
Rev. Sidney A. Lange, S.J.

Introduction

As we set in motion the renewal of the whole Church, we fully recognize how very much depends on the ministry of priests who are the Spirit of Christ. Hence the training of priests is of the greatest importance, and is to reflect the experiences of the past and the spirit and documents of the Council as well as the changed conditions of our times.

CHAPTER I

1. Priestly formation programs are to be formed by the Bishops of each country and approved by papal authority. The reason for this is that cultures are very different, and therefore the approach to the ministry of these people should suit their needs. The approval of the Pope is necessary in order to preserve basic unity.

CHAPTER II

On Promoting Vocations

2. Everyone in the Christian community should foster vocations by a full Christian life, especially in the family. Parish life with the young people involved as fully as possible is also a great means of attracting young men to the priesthood.

Teachers and Catholic associations should strive to foster a climate in which the young man is able and willing to answer the divine call. If the young man sees a priest who is holy, zealous, and happy because he has a purpose in life, he will find the priestly vocation more appealing.

Such cooperation depends on divine Providence, and by the guidance and leadership of lawful ministers of the Church. Prayer, penance, and instruction, especially through the communications media are ways of teaching and forming young people in the excellence of the priestly vocation. All pastoral activity should be handled and unified by vocational organizations in the territories of dioceses, regions, and nations. Good judgment should be used in fostering these activities, and they should not neglect appropriate help from modern psychology and sociology.

Efforts on behalf of vocations should respond to the needs of the whole Church, which means that diocese, religious community, and nation sacrifice for the good of the Church.

3. In minor seminaries there should be special religious formation, emphasizing spiritual direction so that the student will be conditioned to follow Christ. He should lead a normal healthy life, physically and psychologically. The course in the minor seminary should be such that should he decide on another vocation, he could continue his education without any disadvantages. Active concern must be had for men pursuing a vocation later in life.

CHAPTER III
Programming of Major Seminaries

4. Major seminaries ought to develop true shepherds of souls after the model of Jesus Christ, Teacher, Priest, and Shepherd. They must be prepared in the ministry of

the Word, which must be grasped through meditation and expressed in word and action. Likewise they must be prepared to be shepherds and know how to represent Christ before men. They must be prepared "not to be served but to serve" (Mk. 10:45) as Jesus did, and by this service win over many more (1 Cor. 9:19).

Therefore every program of instruction whether spiritual, intellectual, or disciplinary should be made practical for a pastoral ministry.

5. Seminary teachers should be chosen from the best, because good training depends on good teachers who are prepared by solid doctrine and pastoral experience. These teachers should also be trained for spiritual direction.

Seminary directors and teachers must be aware of how much their thinking and acting influences their students. Under the head of the seminary (Rector) there should be harmony in spirit and behavior. The teachers and students of the seminary should strive to be a family, just as Jesus taught His Apostles: "that they may be one" (Jn. 17:11). The bishop should show interest in the seminary, and all priests should regard the seminary as the heart of the diocese.

6. The seminarian should be examined about the rightness of his intention and the freedom of his choice, his spiritual, moral, and intellectual fitness for the priesthood and its pastoral duties.

In selecting and training seminarians, standards must always be firmly maintained, even when there is a shortage of priests.

7. When a diocese must combine its seminarians with the seminarians of another diocese, solid formation must be the supreme law. When seminaries are regional or national, they should be governed by the bishops and endorsed by papal authority.

CHAPTER IV

The Deepening of Spiritual Formation

8. Spiritual formation should be linked with doctrinal and pastoral training. The spiritual father should foster constant companionship with God, the Holy Trinity. Their whole lives should show that they are close friends of Christ the Priest, and this closeness to Christ should inspire in the faithful a closeness to Him. This closeness to Christ should be found in meditation on God's word, in active participation in the mysteries of the Church especially in the Eucharist and the Divine Office, in the Bishop who sends them, and in the people to whom they are sent. They should love and honor the Blessed Virgin Mary, who was given to them as Jesus lay dying on the cross.

The seminarians should earnestly practice these exercises of piety as long as they are in conformity with the practice of solid virtue, especially the virtues of faith, hope, and charity as manifested in the Gospel. By the exercise of these practices they will grow in a spirit of prayer and become effective apostles.

9. Seminarians should be thoroughly penetrated by the mystery of the Church, especially as it has been presented with new clarity in this Council. Priests should therefore be loyal to the Pope and their own bishop, and by working together with their brother priests give witness to the unity of Christ. Seminarians are also to understand that they are called to God's service and pastoral ministry, not to domination or to honors.

If the seminarians are trained in priestly obedience, humility, and self-denial, the result will make them prompt to imitate Christ crucified.

Seminarians must be informed about hardships in their priestly lives, but should also know the saving help of pastoral work itself, which should strengthen their own spiritual lives.

10. Seminarians must be trained carefully to follow priestly celibacy. They must understand that they renounce marriage for the sake of the kingdom of heaven, to manifest an undivided love for God, that they bear witness to the resurrection, and that God provides them with help in their ministry.

Seminarians should be aware of the value and dignity of marriage, but also let them understand the superiority of virginity consecrated to Christ, so that by a mature choice they attach themselves to God by a total gift of body and soul.

Let them be warned of the severe dangers which will confront their chastity today. With divine and human help, let them learn to make the renunciation of marriage for Christ so much a part of their personalities that they will not suffer from celibacy; rather it should lead to a greater mastery of body and soul.

11. The norms for a good Christian education should be maintained and aided by the latest findings in sound psychology and pedagogy. Students should be trained to be mature and emotionally secure. They should be trained in organizing their affairs and prize those qualities which are Christ-like: sincerity, a concern for justice, truthfulness, courtesy of manner, restraint, and kindness.

The discipline of seminary life should not be seen as forced from without, but accepted with personal conviction.

12. The bishops must give the seminarians sufficient time for spiritual training so that their vocation will be decided maturely. It is also good for seminarians to decide if their studies should be interrupted so that they can get pastoral apprenticeship, so that a more rounded test may be made of the priestly candidate. Bishops in certain regions should decide whether the age for ordination to the priesthood should be raised, and whether the seminarian should exercise the office of diaconate for a suitable length of time before being advanced to the priesthood.

CHAPTER V
Revision of Ecclesiastical Studies

13. Before seminarians begin their studies which immediately prepare them for the priesthood, they should be trained in the arts and sciences. They should acquire a command of Latin which will enable them to

understand and use source material for sciences as well as Church documents. The language which the student will use as a priest when he celebrates the liturgy must be mastered, and a suitable knowledge of the languages of Sacred Scripture is required.

14. In the revision of seminary studies, the first object in view must be a better integration of philosophy and theology. These subjects should work together to unfold in the minds of seminarians the mystery of Christ. To accomplish this an introductory course should be given to the students in such a way that the students will see the meaning of their studies. This integration of their studies should help strengthen their personal lives of faith.

15. The purpose of philosophy courses is to give the students an understanding of man, the world, and God. Students should know the everlasting truths of nature as discovered by the light of reason, but they should also know contemporary philosophy which has influence in their own country, and be familiar with recent scientific findings.

The history of philosophy should be so taught, that by coming to grasp with the principles of other systems, students will hold on to what is true, and then be able to detect the roots of error and disprove them.

The system of studies should inspire students to seek and defend the truth vigorously, recognizing the limitations of human understanding. Students should be helped to see the difference between philosophical argument and the mysteries of salvation.

16. "Under the light of faith and with the guidance of the Church's teaching authority, theology should be taught in such a way that students will accurately draw Catholic doctrine from divine revelation, understand that doctrine profoundly, nourish their own spiritual lives with it, and be able to proclaim it, unfold it, and defend it in their priestly ministry."

The study of Sacred Scripture should hold the highest point in the course of theology. After an introduction to Sacred Scripture, the students should learn to some degree the exegetical method, that is, they should understand the circumstances, culture, and frame of mind of the sacred writer. They should also learn the outstanding themes of Sacred Scripture and meditate on them daily.

Dogmatic theology should be so arranged that biblical themes are presented first. Students should see what was handed on by the Church, and understand its relationship to Church history. When these matters are grasped, seminarians should investigate, according to the mind of St. Thomas Aquinas, the deeper meaning, interconnections, and application of these mysteries in liturgy and in human affairs. They should be trained to seek solutions to human problems in the light of revelation and apply the eternal truths to ever changing conditions of humanity in a way that modern man can grasp.

Moral theology also needs to be enriched by Sacred Scripture. It should show the nobility of the Christian vocation, and the nobility of living the life of love it demands. In teaching Canon Law and Church history, the mystery of the Church, as set forth in the Vatican II document on the Church, should be kept in mind.

Students should be led to a better understanding of those churches separated from the Roman Catholic Church so that they will be in a better position to help restore unity among all Christians.

Seminarians should also study non-Christian religions, so that they can better understand the elements of goodness and truth, and learn how to refute errors in them, and to share the full light of truth with those who lack it.

17. Doctrinal training should aim not only at the communication of ideas, but at a genuine formation of students. Hence, teaching methods should be revised to promote a spirit of study among the students.

18. Bishops should see to it that those young men with special qualities be given a chance to develop their abilities whether in scientific method or in the sacred sciences; so that they may better meet the needs of the apostolate.

CHAPTER VI
The Promotion of Strictly Pastoral Training

19. Pastoral concern demands that the seminarians have special training in catechetics, preaching, liturgical worship, the administration of the sacraments, works of charity, the duty of seeking out the straying sheep and unbelievers. Let them receive training in guiding souls so that they can lead

all the "sons of the Church" to a Christian way of life, fulfilled by apostolic action.

In general the seminarians should be trained to listen to other people and lovingly turn to people in their human needs.

20. Following the authority of the Church, let them use the helps of pedagogy, psychology, and sociology to ignite the spark of apostolic zeal in the layman to promote more and successful forms of the apostolate. Students for the priesthood should furthermore be aware of the needs of the universal Church and be ready to preach the Gospel anywhere.

21. Seminarians must learn the needs of the apostolate not only in theory but in practice as well. Hence during their course of studies and vacations, they should be introduced into pastoral practices by suitable activity in real pastoral situations. Above all, let them keep in mind the value of supernatural help.

CHAPTER VII

The Refinement of Training After the Course of Studies

22. Because of modern circumstances, priestly training should be pursued and perfected even after the seminary course has been completed. Therefore seminars, lectures, conferences, and other fitting projects should be designed to help the younger clergy to be gradually introduced into priestly life and activity.

Conclusion

"We, the Fathers of this holy Council, furthering the work begun by the Council of Trent, trustingly confide to seminary directors and teachers the duty of forming Christ's future priests in the spirit of that renewal which this Council has fostered." Those preparing for the priesthood should realize that the hope of the Church and the salvation of souls are being entrusted to them.

Declaration on Christian Education

(Gravissimum Educationis,
October 28, 1965)

A paraphrase by
Rev. Thomas M. Kelly, S.J.

Preface

In carrying out the mission she has received from Christ, the Church has a concern for the whole of man's life, and so has a leading role to play in the progress of man's education. Especially is this true in the present when man, ever more conscious of his dignity and responsibilities, is eager for an active role in building his society. Increasingly people throughout the world devote their energies to building schools, adding greater numbers of those enrolled of all ages, and especially to developing the quality and diversity of educational programs. Accordingly, we propose certain principles concerning Christian education, especially in regard to schools. At the same time, we suggest that in the future a special commission apply these general principles to different local circumstances under the direction of national conferences of bishops.

The Principles

1. All men, by virtue of their dignity as human persons have an inalienable right to education. True education has as its goal, the formation of the individual so as to prepare him for his final destiny and to share as an adult in promoting the welfare of the society in which he lives.

Moreover, education should promote brotherly relations of good will with citizens of other nations, so that true unity and peace may flourish among the peoples of the world.

The young should be educated to develop their physical, moral, and intellectual qualities. Through good education the young will acquire a maturity that will enable them not only to lead responsible lives, but also to take an active part in promoting the common good.

Children also have a right to a training which will develop within them moral values and a correct conscience. Their knowledge and love of God must be a goal of education. Those with public authority should not deny the young this sacred right.

2. Since every Christian has become a new creature by rebirth from water and the Holy Spirit, so that he may be called what he truly is, a child of God, he is entitled to a Christian education. For this basic reason Christian education has a further aim of making the baptized aware of the mystery of salvation as well as the gift of faith. Spiritual formation includes a teaching of how to worship, especially in liturgical action. As the Christian advances in his educational development, he should be a witness of Christ and be conscious of his part in transforming the world with the spirit and teachings of Christ.

3. Parents are the primary and principal educators of their children. Parents should create a family atmosphere animated by love and respect for both God and fellow men. It is within the family context that the young child is taught about God, to worship Him, and to love his neighbor.

The family needs help from society in the task of educating. Thus, certain rights and duties belong to civil society to direct what is required for the common good. Civil society promotes education in many ways, namely: to protect the duties and rights of parents, to give them aid when it is needed, and, moreover, to build schools and institutions as the common good demands.

The Church also shares in the duty of educating the young. She must promote a training by which the spirit of Christ will imbue their complete life.

4. Catechetical instruction is foremost among the means the Church uses to accomplish her educational role. Such instructions seek to: strengthen faith, nourish a spiritual life, encourage an active participation in the liturgy, and foster apostolic activity. The Church values highly all media of social communication and seeks to enoble them by informing them with her own spirit.

5. The school by its friendly atmosphere encourages mutual understanding among pupils of diverse backgrounds and constitutes a center for joint participation of families, teachers, various kinds of cultural, civic, religious groups, and the entire community. Since the school has the greatest potential for advancing the intellectual and spiritual growth of the young, educators have a serious and special vocation. A teacher's vocation demands special qualities of mind and heart and a continuing readiness to renew and to adapt.

6. Parents have the true liberty in their choice of school for their children. Consequently, the government is obliged to defend this parental right. Furthermore, public assistance is to be given in such a way that

parents are truly free to choose the schools they want for their children.

Following the principle of subsidiarity, so that no kind of school monopoly arises, it is the task of the State to protect the right of the children to adequate school education, check on the ability of the teachers, look after the health of the pupils, and, in general, promote the entire work of the school.

7. The Church has a serious obligation to provide religious and moral education for those students attending other than Catholic schools.

Parents, for their part, are obliged to a concern for the Christian formation of their children. The Church is deeply grateful to those civil authorities which, showing due respect for religious freedom, insure that the education in the schools is given according to the moral and religious convictions of each family.

8. The Catholic school aims to create a school community animated by the Gospel spirit of freedom and charity. The Church's role in education is manifested especially in the Catholic school which has as its overall aim to relate all human culture to the message of salvation. The Catholic school, in view of present day conditions of an age of progress, so prepares its pupils that the Catholic graduate by living an exemplary and apostolic life may become the saving yeast of the human family. The Catholic school retains its vital importance especially in the circumstances of our times and so we proclaim again the

right of the Church freely to establish and operate schools of every kind and at every level.

The on-going strength of the Catholic schools lies in its teachers. They are to be aware of its goals and programs. Teachers are to be given adequate preparation for their task. Their pedagogical skills are not enough. The apostolic vocation of the teacher needs to be based on the virtue of charity demonstrated to each other and to their pupils. We exhort all to an active support of Catholic education. Parents are urged to send their youngsters to Catholic schools whenever possible.

9. The Catholic school system is encouraged to expand into other areas of special education. There is a need to become involved in the fields of technical and professional schools for adult education. Other services to be rendered by the Catholic school would be "special education" for the retarded and training institutes for teachers of religion.

Once again, pastors of the Church, and the faithful should be generous in helping the schools to become more effective, especially in caring for the poor, the orphans, and for those who do not have the faith.

10. Catholic colleges and universities must be vigilant that higher studies are to be pursued with an academic freedom and a scientific inquiry. Scholars, following the example of St. Thomas Aquinas, can come to fuller realization of the harmony between faith and science.

In those Catholic universities where there is no school of divinity, there should be an institute or department of sacred sciences which can provide for the needs of the lay students.

Catholic universities should be strategically distributed throughout the world. They should distinguish themselves not for the number of students enrolled but for the manifest excellence of their academic achievements.

Pastors of souls and bishops must provide for the spiritual welfare of Catholic students attending State and other universities. Catholic centers on these campuses, if staffed by especially trained priests, religious, and laymen, should be centers of guidance, both spiritual and intellectual.

11. Seminaries are a great benefit to the Church. To them is entrusted the priestly formation of the students. Further, they prepare future teachers and promote research in the different fields of sacred learning. Their objectives also include a constant and deeper understanding of sacred revelation and a respect for Christian wisdom of former generations. Through dialogue with separated brethren and with non-Christians, solutions will be discovered to a whole range of problems, including the one regarding the development of doctrine.

12. Coordination and cooperation are essential in our times both within the faculties of the same university and between other schools. This should be developed as the welfare of the whole community requires. This, at times, will require a sharing of the scientific research between disciplines and the temporary exchange of professors.

Conclusion

The whole task of education is of such importance that we encourage young people to consider teaching as a vocation, especially in those countries where the youth may be denied an education because of the lack of teachers. We also wish to express our deep gratitude to all teachers who have devoted themselves to the work of education at all levels.

Decree on the Instruments of Social Communication

(*Inter Mirifica*, December 4, 1963)

A paraphrase by
Rev. Frederick J. Buckley

1. By God's will human ingenuity has produced in our times marvelous technical inventions. Some of these make available new and especially effective ways of communicating every type of idea, news, or guidance. The Church as a mother, gladly receives these inventions and observes them with special care. Of particular concern are those means of communication which of their very nature can touch and affect not merely individual persons but also the masses and even the entire human community. These are the press, motion pictures, radio and television. They are rightly called instruments of social communication.

2. Mother Church realizes that if these media are properly used they can nourish the human family with health-giving food. They can make a real contribution to the renewal and development of the human spirit and to the extension and upbuilding of God's kingdom. However, the Church knows that these gifts can be used in a way contrary to God's Will and harmful to mankind. Indeed, as a mother, the Church is deeply distressed at the injury all too frequently inflicted on society by the wrong use of these media.

Therefore, sharing the concern of popes and bishops in a matter of such seriousness, we feel obliged to deal with the central problems posed by the media of social communication. As a Council we are confident that the principles and directives we set forth will benefit not only Christians but the entire human family.

CHAPTER I

3. The Church has the commission from Christ to proclaim the Gospel and bring salvation to all people. Therefore it is part of her duty both to preach the good news with the help of these powerful media of social communication and to instruct mankind in their proper use. Hence the Church claims as a basic right the use and possession of all instruments of this type which are necessary or useful in forming Christians and in working for man's salvation.

Pastors ought to offer guidance to their people in the right use of the media, and laymen involved in the media ought to try to enliven these instruments with a humane and Christian spirit.

4. In determining what makes for a proper use of the media it is necessary to take into account a number of circumstances such as the audience, the time, the place, the intention, and the subject matter. It is necessary also to consider how a given instrument of the media achieves its effect. Sometimes a powerful effect results from indirect persuasion, one that people are unable to detect or deal with.

5. The search for news and the publication of news presents special problems. There exists a right to that information which will enable people actively to contribute to the common good. However the news must be as true and complete as charity and justice allow, and the manner of communication should befit human dignity.

6.-7. Art must respect the moral law, that is, man in his total nature as God's reasoning creature called to eternal life. The description and presentation of moral evil should be done in such a way as to lead to a deeper understanding of man and the value of truth and goodness. Moral norms are needed in the treatment of subject matter which all too easily triggers fallen man's basest desires.

8.-9. Since public opinion is so powerful today, each person has a duty to form and express sound views on public affairs. There is a special duty on the part of a listener, viewer, or reader to use good judgment in supporting good programs and publications and to seek guidance of competent authorities in their selection.

10. All people, especially young people, should exercise self-control and self-discipline in using discernment regarding what they see, hear and read. Parents have a special obligation to be aware of shows or publications that undermine truth and goodness, and then take measures to protect against them.

11. The chief responsibility for the proper use of the media rests upon those who actively promote their use, such as newsmen, writers, actors, producers, distributors, critics, etc. Professional groups ought to draw up and enforce codes of ethical conduct for their own members. Of special concern are the needs of young people who need good entertainment and inspiration. Religious themes should be handled with due reverence and with competence.

12. The civil government has a special duty in relation to the general welfare to see to it that serious danger to public morals and social progress does not result from a

perverted use of these instruments. It is the duty of civil authority to foster and protect a true and just availability of information since the progress of modern society depends on this. Furthermore, it should foster religion, culture, and the fine arts, and protect consumers in the free exercise of their rights.

CHAPTER II

13. Now is the time for all the People of God to put a really serious effort into using the media for spreading God's word. The state of the world cries out for apostolic zeal in this direction. Christian laymen have a real obligation to put their technical skill, their money and their abilities into this effort of giving witness to Christ through the use of these modern media which reach so many people with such forceful impact.

14. There is need to set up and support an effective Catholic press to give a Christian interpretation about what is happening in the world and in the Church. The production, distribution and showing of motion pictures which are worthwhile ought to be supported and commended. Since radio and television programs can lead people to share in the light and truth of Christ, efforts should be made to establish Catholic stations. Their offerings should excel in professional quality.

The art of the theatre, which can reach vast audiences through the media, should be revived, for it can help people grow culturally and spiritually.

15.-16. In order to use these instruments for the spread of the Gospel, priests, Religious and laymen need to be trained in the required technical skills. There is a need for schools animated by a Christian spirit where movie, radio and television writers, actors, critics, etc., can get a well rounded formation. Since audiences vary in age and cultural background, Catholic schools at every level should include instructions on the right use of the media.

17. The very great expense and the technical problems involved, especially in television, should not be allowed to silence or slow down the word of salvation. There is a serious obligation before God to support radio and television programs and stations whose main purpose is to proclaim the Gospel and build up the body of Christ. Accordingly we urge those groups or individuals of great wealth to give generously and willingly to make possible the rapid and forceful spread of God's Word.

18. The Church's apostolate in this whole area of the social communication media calls for immediate vigorous action. Let each diocese urge the people to pray and make a contribution toward this holy cause.

19.-22. The supreme pastoral responsibility regarding the media rests with the Holy Father through the Pontifical Commission for Social Communications. Within his own diocese it is the Bishop's duty to oversee, promote, and regulate the social communication apostolate. To unify plans and efforts in this apostolate we as a Council direct that in each country a national office for press, motion pictures, radio, and televison be established. This office should be under a special commission of bishops or some delegate-bishop and make use of knowledgeable laymen. Where the influence of these media extends beyond the national borders, the national offices should cooperate together in an international effort.

23. We decree that a pastoral instruction be drawn up under the supervision of the Pontifical Commission for Social Communications Media. If the members of the Church follow the guidelines faithfully, they will avoid problems and difficulties and do their part to light the world with the light of Christ.

24. Since the fate of the human race is increasingly more dependent on the right use of these media, we the Council Fathers urge all men of goodwill, particularly those who control these instruments, to strive to apply them solely for the good of mankind. Thus the name of the Lord will be glorified by modern technology.

THE CONTRIBUTORS

The Rev. Gregory John Andrews was ordained a priest for the Diocese of St. Petersburg in 1976 after attaining two master of theology degrees at St. Vincent de Paul Major Seminary, Boynton Beach, Florida. As associate pastor of St. Cecilia Parish in Clearwater, Florida, he conducts programs for youth and programs in religious education and in liturgy.

The Rev. Frederick J. Buckley, who holds an M.S.W. from Boston College, conducts a weekly radio program, "Religion Today" and on station WLCY-TV, Tampa, Florida, a series called "The Pastor's Study." After his ordination in 1945 in Boston he was professor of sociology and psychology at St. John's Seminary School of Theology at Brighton, Massachusetts and served as Assistant Director of the Catholic Charitable Bureau. He conducted a series of talks on "Religion and Psychoanalysis" on the Catholic Hour.

The Rev. Harold B. Bumpus, Doctor of Theology, distinguished Professor of Catholic Studies, St. Leo College, St. Leo, Florida, is also Director of Clergy, Education and Ecumenism as well as Vicar for Religious of the Diocese of St. Petersburg. Holding degrees in chemistry, philosophy, and theology (University of Tuebingen, 1969), he has taught History of Doctrine and courses in dogmatics at Weston College and Episcopal Theological School, Weston, Mass.

The Rev. Robert Ference, a native of Pennsylvania, was educated in New Jersey and graduated from Duquesne University. On March 21, 1965, he was ordained to the priesthood for the Byzantine Catholic Eparchy of Passaic, N.J., and in June of that year received the S.T.L. from Catholic University. Presently he is pastor of St. Therese Church in St. Petersburg, Florida, and serves on the Ecumenical and Interreligious Affairs Commission of the diocese.

Mr. Robert C. Gibbons, J.D., formerly an associate of the law firm of Gibbons, Tucker, McEwen, Smith, Cofer and Taub of Tampa, Florida, was educated at Emory University where he graduated with high honors in history before going on to law school at the University of Florida. He is currently studying for the priesthood at St. Vincent de Paul Major Seminary, Boynton Beach, Florida.

The Rev. Ernest J. Jacques, S.J. is a scripture scholar trained in biblical studies at the Gregorian University in Rome. He was ordained to the priesthood in 1966. He is professor of theology on the faculty of Spring Hill College, Mobile, Alabama.

The Rev. Thomas M. Kelly, S.J. ordained to the priesthood in 1957 is presently associate pastor of Sacred Heart Parish in Tampa, Florida. He has had extensive experience in the field of education having been a teacher and counselor at Jesuit high schools in New Orleans, La., Shreveport, La., and Tampa, Florida. He also held a post in administration at Loyola University in New Orleans, La.

The Rev. Sidney A. Lange, S.J., since his ordination to the priesthood in 1962 has had wide experience in teaching and pastoral ministry. After having served in parishes in Dallas, Albuquerque and New Orleans, he is the present pastor of Sacred Heart Parish, Tampa, Florida, and Catholic Chaplain of Tampa University. He is a member of the Senate of Priests and of the Catechetical Commission of the Diocese of St. Petersburg.

Sister M. Jerome Leavy, O.S.B., Prioress of the Benedictine Sisters of Florida, is a member of the Board of Trustees of St. Leo College, St. Leo, Florida, and brings to her position twenty years teaching and administration at the elementary, high school, and college levels. She is a member of the Leadership Conference of Women Religious and formerly on the President's Council of the Federation of St. Scholastica.

The Rev. Clement J. McNaspy, S.J., author, lecturer, and teacher, and University Professor, Loyola University, New Orleans, La., is one of the foremost liturgical scholars in the United States and a charter member of the North American Academy of Liturgy. He has written several books on the liturgy: *Our Changing Liturgy*, *Worship and Witness*, and *What A Modern Catholic Believes About Worship*. He authored the special commentary on the "Constitution on the Sacred Liturgy" in the Abbott Edition of *The Documents of Vatican II*. He is featured in *Who's Who of American Catholics*.

The Rev. Austin N. Park, S.J., is an associate pastor of the Immaculate Conception Church in downtown New Orleans, La. Upon completion of his theological studies in Oña, Spain, and his ordination in 1955, he engaged in parish work both in Florida and in El Paso, Texas. A leader in social reform, he was the co-founder of Metropolitan Ministries in Tampa, Florida, a service facility for the indigent.

The Rev. Norman J. Rogge, S.J., has spent most of his twenty years of priestly service in parish work, nearly all of it in Tampa, Florida, at Sacred Heart Parish where he is associate pastor. His ministry has been mainly with the most deprived persons of human society. He also teaches religion in the parish elementary school where he serves as chaplain.

Marina E. Ruffolo was born in Milan, Italy, where she was educated by the Ursuline Sisters. She attended Hofstra College, New York, as well as St. Mary's, Winona, Minnesota, with a special interest in languages. After a laborious and meticulous study of the sixteen Documents of Vatican II, she realized the vital importance of disseminating these treasures in a paraphrase that could be appreciated by all men. It was her remarkable insight into the importance and potential impact on all the faithful that was responsible for initiating and completing this work. Marina Ruffolo is the wife of a Tampa, Florida, physician and mother of three children.

Sister Mary Gregoria Rush, O.S.F. is presently the Ministerial Coordinator of the Sisters Advisory Council of the Diocese of St. Petersburg. Her professional training has been in music with a Masters Degree in Music from the University of Indiana and graduate studies at Eastman School of Music; in communications with courses at University of Boulder, Colorado; and in gerontology after training at the University of South Florida. She has been a teacher, organist, choir director in various parishes in Iowa and Florida.

The Rev. Simon E. Smith, S.J., took his degree in scripture from Harvard Divinity School. Before ordination in 1961 he taught for a year and studied Arabic for two years at Baghdad College in Iraq. He taught Scripture and Theology in the Continuing Education programs of the dioceses of Bridgeport and Worcester and was Instructor in Liturgy both at Boston College School of Philosophy and at Weston School of Theology. For thirteen years he was an editor of *New Testament Abstracts* and made archaeological excavations in Israel in two successive years. Now he is the Executive Secretary of Jesuit Missions, Inc. and Director of Horizons for Justice Program. He serves on the boards of Jesuit Missions, Inc., Jesuit Volunteer Corps East, and the United States Mission Council. He is a charter member of the American Society of Missiology and serves on its Executive Committee.

The Rev. John R. Welsh, S.J., who holds a degree in sacred liturgy, has been an educator all of his priestly life since ordination in 1956;

religion teacher, department chairman of religion, and President of Jesuit High School in Shreveport, La. He has devoted much of his time to the reform of adult and juvenile correction systems in Louisiana by founding several organizations and programs in that field. Presently he heads the theology department at Jesuit High School in Tampa, Florida.

Daughters of St. Paul

IN MASSACHUSETTS
 50 St. Paul's Ave. Jamaica Plain, Boston, MA 02130;
  617-522-8911; 617-522-0875;
 172 Tremont Street, Boston, MA 02111; **617-426-5464;
  617-426-4230**
IN NEW YORK
 78 Fort Place, Staten Island, NY 10301; **212-447-5071**
 59 East 43rd Street, New York, NY 10017; **212-986-7580**
 7 State Street, New York, NY 10004; **212-447-5071**
 625 East 187th Street, Bronx, NY 10458; **212-584-0440**
 525 Main Street, Buffalo, NY 14203; **716-847-6044**
IN NEW JERSEY
 Hudson Mall — Route 440 and Communipaw Ave.,
  Jersey City, NJ 07304; **201-433-7740**
IN CONNECTICUT
 202 Fairfield Ave., Bridgeport, CT 06604; **203-335-9913**
IN OHIO
 2105 Ontario St. (at Prospect Ave.), Cleveland, OH 44115; **216-621-9427**
 25 E. Eighth Street, Cincinnati, OH 45202; **513-721-4838**
IN PENNSYLVANIA
 1719 Chestnut Street, Philadelphia, PA 19103; **215-568-2638**
IN FLORIDA
 2700 Biscayne Blvd., Miami, FL 33137; **305-573-1618**
IN LOUISIANA
 4403 Veterans Memorial Blvd., Metairie, LA 70002; **504-887-7631;
  504-887-0113**
 1800 South Acadian Thruway, P.O. Box 2028, Baton Rouge, LA 70821
  504-343-4057; 504-343-3814
IN MISSOURI
 1001 Pine Street (at North 10th), St. Louis, MO 63101; **314-621-0346;
  314-231-1034**
IN ILLINOIS
 172 North Michigan Ave., Chicago, IL 60601; **312-346-4228**
IN TEXAS
 114 Main Plaza, San Antonio, TX 78205; **512-224-8101**
IN CALIFORNIA
 1570 Fifth Avenue, San Diego, CA 92101; **714-232-1442**
 46 Geary Street, San Francisco, CA 94108; **415-781-5180**
IN HAWAII
 1143 Bishop Street, Honolulu, HI 96813; **808-521-2731**
IN ALASKA
 750 West 5th Avenue, Anchorage AK 99501; **907-272-8183**
IN CANADA
 3022 Dufferin Street, Toronto 395, Ontario, Canada
IN ENGLAND
 128, Notting Hill Gate, London W11 3QG, England
133 Corporation Street, Birmingham B4 6PH, England
5A-7 Royal Exchange Square, Glasgow G1 3AH, England
82 Bold Street, Liverpool L1 4HR, England
IN AUSTRALIA
 58 Abbotsford Rd., Homebush, N.S.W., Sydney 2140, Australia